Learns to Bake

S.T.E.A.M. Holiday Cookbook
for Kids 4-12

AJ Kikumoto

Copyright © 2023- AJ Kikumoto

Aaliyah, Akyra, Amaya, Akayla, CJ, and Alyvia Kikumoto

All rights reserved. No part of this book may be used or reproduced in any manner without direct written permission from the author or the publisher.

Published by: Queen Publishing Agency

Images used under license from depositphotos.com and pexels.com

Please be careful when using knives, scissors, and any sharp objects described in this book. The author is not liable for any accidents or misuse of such items. Only adults should use sharp objects. Please be careful with permanent markers such as black Sharpies. They will stain.

Discover the royal treatment at Queen Publishing Agency, where we bring your work to life with unparalleled quality and timeless class, ensuring that you retain full ownership of all royalties. Explore our services and embark on your publishing journey with us at QueenPublishingAgency.com!

**As a special gift for purchasing this book,
grab your FREEbie at linktr.ee/AJKikumoto**

Collect all our books!

Visit us at www.AJKikumoto.com and www.QueenPublishingAgency.com

Be Social! Follow us on social media and tag us in your masterpieces!
@AJKikumoto

For information, address Queen Publishing Agency:
hello@queenpublishingagency.com

ISBN: 978-1-953556-28-8

Dedicated to my everything! All my little bakers!

TABLE OF CONTENTS

Introduction

Chapter 1 11
STEAM (Science, Technology, Engineering, Arts, Math) in Baking

Chapter 2 22
100+ STEAM Activities You Can Eat!

Chapter 3 66
Baking Basics for Young Bakers

Chapter 4 74
Morning Magic: Breakfast Bites and STEAM Delights

Chapter 5 84
Cookie Creativity: STEAM-infused Christmas Delights for Young Bakers

Chapter 6 93
Cookie Creativity: STEAM- infused
Christmas Delights - Gingerbread

Chapter 7 118
Swift Sweets: Speedy STEAM Treats
to Sparkle Up Your Holidays

Chapter 8 125
Conversions & Equivalents

Chapter 9 127
BONUS! Holiday Dad Jokes

Chapter 10 140
STEAM Challenge Planner, STEAM
Exploration, Fraction Chart, Math:
Double That Recipe, My Recipe
Template

INTRODUCTION

In the exciting world of STEAM, we add "Art" to STEM's foundation of Science, Technology, Engineering, and Math. So, while STEM focuses on the technical, STEAM brings creativity to the mix, turning science and technology into a delightful masterpiece, just like a well-crafted recipe in our holiday cookbook!

In our household, Christmas memories and traditions hold a special place. We continually seek fresh ideas to enhance our time-honored events. From the delightful scent of freshly baked sugar cookies to the joyful mess of sprinkles adorning the floor during cookie decorating, crafting gingerbread houses or trains bound for the North Pole, to the cherished moments of family relaxation watching Christmas movies all night with a bucket of hot buttered popcorn—these are the traditions that we hold dear in our home.

Welcome to the enchanting world of our Children's Holiday Cookbook, where we sprinkle magic into your family's Christmas traditions! Have fun with the 100+ STEAM Activities you can eat, the breakfasts, cookies, and quick treats to bake with your children quickly, and enjoy a good, clean holiday dad joke. This book is for you! Turn on your favorite Christmas Carols and sing along as you celebrate old traditions and make new ones with your family. So, while STEM lays the foundation, STEAM adds a splash of creativity, turning learning into a delightful and well-rounded experience for curious minds!

So, let's whip up some festive treats that stimulate the mind and ignite the creative spark within! Elevate your

holiday traditions with our delightful recipes, creating moments that will linger in your family's heart for years to come!

Possibly the most important word in the dictionary is "remember." Remember your family. Remember your traditions. Remember the Lord. As we finish the journey of one year and cross the bridge to the following year, let us remember the true Giver. He who brings joy to the world. The Light of the World. The birth of the Saviour is always a reason to rejoice. "Good tidings of great joy... to all people." Luke 2:10.

Chapter 1

S.T.E.A.M. (Science, Technology, Engineering, Arts, Math) in Baking

STEM vs STEAM

STEM is like a superhero Science, Technology, Engineering, and Math team. But, when we add "A" for Art to make STEAM, it's like giving our superhero team extra powers. In our Holiday STEAM cookbook, we use STEAM because it's like having magical ingredients that make baking yummy and a super fun adventure where we can be creative and learn cool things about everything – from mixing ingredients to designing tasty treats!

In our Holiday STEAM cookbook, we use STEAM because baking isn't just about following recipes—it's also about exploring the artistic side of making delicious treats. So, with

STEAM, we have all the cool science, tech, math, and the magic of art to make our recipes extra memorable and fun!

SCIENCE

Baking is a delicious science experiment for young chefs, where they discover how ingredients transform through chemical reactions, witness dough rising like magic with the help of yeast, and explore the fascinating world of measurements affecting the final tasty outcome in our cookbook.

We can learn how ingredients like yeast change and react and the importance of precise measurements.

TECHNOLOGY

Technology becomes our kitchen wizard in our baking adventure, guiding us through recipes with interactive apps, smart appliances, and fun gadgets. From using tablets to follow step-by-step instructions to exploring how ovens and mixers work, technology in our cookbook for kids makes baking an exciting blend of creativity and innovation!

We can use mixers, ovens, smart appliances, and fun gadgets to blend creativity and innovation.

ENGINEERING

In our cookbook for budding bakers, engineering skills come alive as kids design and build edible masterpieces. From crafting sturdy gingerbread houses to assembling layered cakes, each recipe is a tasty opportunity for young engineers to unleash their creativity in the kitchen.

We can design and build edible masterpieces and unleash our creativity in the kitchen.

ARTS

In our cookbook for young bakers, the artistry of baking unfolds like a canvas of flavors and colors. From decorating cookies with vibrant icings to sculpting edible creations, each recipe is an invitation for kids to express their creativity, turning the kitchen into their own delightful art studio.

We can express our creativity by turning the kitchen into an art studio, decorating cookies, and sculpting edible creations.

MATH

Every recipe becomes a delicious equation to solve in our cookbook for young baking mathematicians. From measuring ingredients with precision to understanding ratios in recipes, each step becomes a delightful equation, making baking a tasty way to explore the wonders of mathematics. Math is the secret ingredient that turns the kitchen into a fun learning space.

We can measure ingredients precisely and understand recipes' ratios as each step becomes a delightful equation.

WHAT MAKES THIS COOKBOOK DIFFERENT FROM THE OTHER COOKBOOKS?

These additions make our cookbook educational and a delightful and immersive experience for young chefs exploring the world of baking and STEAM.

- **Edible Science Experiments:**
  - Simple, safe, and edible science experiments related to cooking and baking.

- **Math in the Kitchen:**
  - Basic math concepts are integrated into some of the recipes, like measuring ingredients, dividing portions, and understanding cooking times. This not only enhances baking skills but also reinforces mathematical concepts in a practical way.

Creative Food Art:

- Artistic expression is encouraged by incorporating food art projects. We teach kids to turn ordinary ingredients into fun and festive creations, fostering creativity and presentation skills.

Storytelling Recipes:

- Storytelling is introduced with some recipes. Narratives are created around the origin of a dish, its cultural significance, or the journey of ingredients from farm to table. This adds an educational and engaging element to the cookbook.

Seasonal Ingredient Exploration:

- Seasonal ingredients and their availability, along with information about the benefits of eating seasonally and how they impact the environment, are introduced.

Food Geography:

- The geographical origins of various dishes are explored. Recipes connect to different regions, cultures, and traditions, providing a global perspective on holiday cooking.

Baking Safety Tips:

- Age-appropriate cooking safety tips are incorporated by emphasizing the importance of kitchen hygiene, handling utensils, and understanding basic kitchen tools.

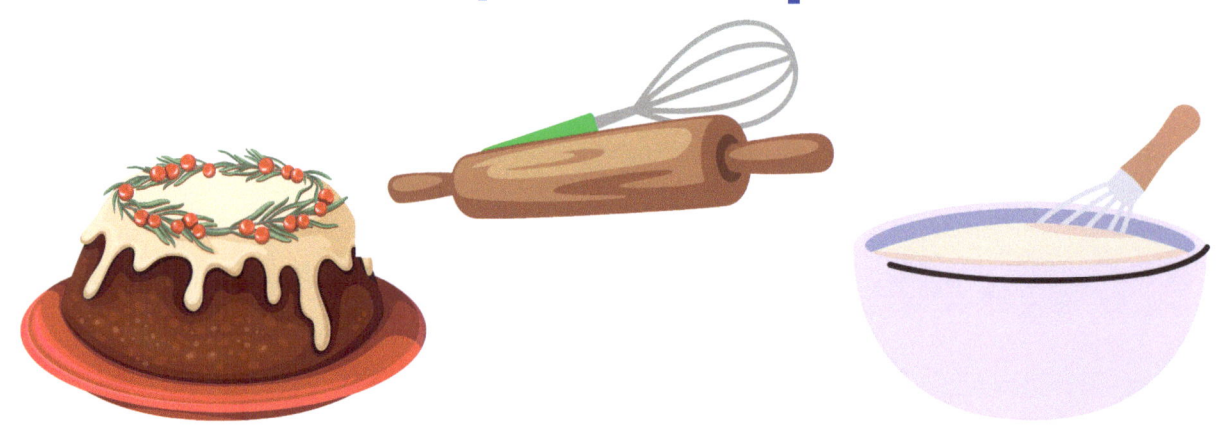

November 8
INTERNATIONAL
STEAM DAY

SCIENCE. TECHNOLOGY. ENGINEERING. ARTS. MATHEMATICS

Inspire student chefs to think creatively, collaborate, and solve problems.

WE ARE ALL MAKERS N BAKERS

S — **Let's learn about Science!**
We can learn how ingredients like yeast change and react and the importance of precise measurements.

T — **Let's learn about Technology!**
We can use mixers, ovens, smart appliances, and fun gadgets for an exciting blend of creativity and innovation.

E — **Let's learn about Engineering!**
We can design and build edible masterpieces and unleash our creativity in the kitchen.

A — **Let's learn about Art!**
We can express our creativity by turning the kitchen into an art studio, decorating cookies, and sculpting edible creations.

M — **Let's learn about Math!**
We can measure ingredients precisely and understand recipes' ratios as each step becomes a delightful equation.

LEARNING THROUGH STEAM

By integrating these five areas, kid bakers are empowered to explore, innovate, and thrive in an ever-evolving world.

SCIENCE:
- Encourages curiosity and a deep understanding of the natural world.
- Provides a foundation for inquiry-based learning and scientific thinking.
- Sparks creativity by inspiring kid bakers to explore and question the unknown.

TECHNOLOGY:
- Equips kid bakers with the skills to navigate the digital age.
- Promotes computational thinking and problem-solving abilities.
- Cultivates creativity by empowering kid bakers to design and develop digital solutions.

ENGINEERING:
- Develops critical thinking and analytical skills.
- Encourages kid bakers to design and create solutions to real-world problems.
- Fosters teamwork, perseverance, and a growth mindset.

ARTS:
- Provides a platform for self-expression and creativity.
- Enhances imagination and fosters innovative thinking.
- Promotes interdisciplinary collaboration by bridging STEM fields with artistic expression.

MATHEMATICS:
- Cultivates logical reasoning and quantitative analysis skills.
- Encourages creative thinking by applying mathematical concepts to real-world scenarios.
- Stimulates innovation by using mathematical modeling and algorithms.

Embracing the power of STEAM nurtures creativity, inspires lifelong learning, and equips kid bakers with the skills needed to thrive in the 21st century.

STEAM ALPHABET

A	B	C	D	E
Art	Biology	Construct	Design	Engineering

F	G	H	I	J	K
Food	Gears	Hypothesis	Invent	Jupiter	Knowledge

L	M	N	O	P
Language	Mathematics	Nature	Orbit	Plan

Q	R	S	T	U
Questions	Robotics	Science	Technology	Universe

V	W	X	Y	Z
Volcano	Wind Energy	X-Ray	Yeast	Zones

Chapter 2

100+ STEAM Activities You Can Eat!

Welcome, creative minds, to a world where Science, Technology, Engineering, Art, and Mathematics (STEAM) come together in over 100 edible activities! 🌟

In this section, our goal is to spark curiosity and ignite your imagination. Each activity description is intentionally minimal, inviting you to explore, discover, and let your artistic instincts flourish. You might need to use your smartphone or tablet to look up a YouTube video or a detailed process.

Edible STEAM is not just about learning—it's about the joy of creating, experimenting, and savoring the delicious results.

I encourage you to share your edible masterpieces with the world! Post your creations on social media and follow/tag **@ajkikumoto** and **@zoeysgreatadventures**. Let's build a community of innovative taste-makers! 🌈

As for me, choosing a favorite activity is like picking the sweetest fruit from a vast orchard—it's tough! But I'd love to hear about your favorites. Let the edible adventures begin! 🍏🎨🧁

Happy exploring, experimenting, and, of course, snacking! 🍭🔍🎨 #EdibleSTEAM #zoeysgreatadventures

STEAM ACTIVITIES YOU CAN EAT AGES 4-8

- 1. **Gingerbread Man Geometry:**

    - Ingredients: Gingerbread cookie dough, icing, assorted candies
    - Directions: Roll out the dough and cut gingerbread men. Decorate with candies, discussing shapes and symmetry. (30 minutes)

2. Candy Cane Science:

- Ingredients: Candy canes
- Directions: Observe what happens when you dip candy canes in hot cocoa versus cold milk. Discuss states of matter. (15 minutes)

3. Edible Snowflakes:

- Ingredients: Pretzel sticks, mini marshmallows, white chocolate
- Directions: Create snowflakes by arranging pretzel sticks and mini marshmallows, then drizzle with melted white chocolate. Discuss symmetry. (20 minutes)

4. Christmas Tree Engineering:

- Ingredients: Sugar cones, green icing, assorted candies
- Directions: Decorate sugar cones as Christmas trees using candies. Discuss engineering concepts like balance and stability. (25 minutes)

5. Jingle Bell Sound Patterns:

- Ingredients: Jingle bells, different containers
- Directions: Experiment with different containers filled with jingle bells to create sound patterns. Discuss sound waves. (15 minutes)

6. Colorful Candy Experiments:

- Ingredients: Skittles, water, white plate
- Directions: Arrange Skittles around the edge of a plate, pour warm water in the center, and observe the color diffusion. Discuss color mixing. (20 minutes)

7. Holiday Ice Sculptures:

- Ingredients: Water, holiday-shaped molds, food coloring (optional)
- Directions: Freeze water in holiday-shaped molds. Discuss states of matter and observe melting. (4 hours, including freezing time)

8. Snowman Melting Moments:

- Ingredients: Marshmallows, chocolate chips, pretzel sticks
- Directions: Use marshmallows and chocolate chips to build snowmen, then observe them "melt" in a warm environment. Discuss heat transfer. (20 minutes)

9. Christmas Cookie Sorting:

- Ingredients: Various shaped cookies
- Directions: Sort cookies by shape, size, or color. Discuss sorting and categorization. (15 minutes)

10. Peppermint Playdough Chemistry:

- Ingredients: Peppermint extract, red food coloring, playdough ingredients
- Directions: Make peppermint-scented playdough and discuss chemical reactions. (30 minutes)

11. Cranberry Counting Structures:

- Ingredients: Toothpicks, cranberries
- Directions: Use cranberries and toothpicks to build structures while practicing counting and basic geometry. (25 minutes)

12. Holiday/Peppermint Volcanoes:

- Ingredients: Baking soda, vinegar, red and green food coloring
- Directions: Create a holiday-themed volcano by combining baking soda and vinegar. Add Peppermint extract if desired for that yummy holiday smell. Discuss chemical reactions. Use your smartphone to search for a How-To video on YouTube. (20 minutes)

13. Edible Symmetry with Sandwiches:

- Ingredients: Bread, various spreads, toppings
- Directions: Create symmetrical sandwiches using different spreads and toppings. Discuss symmetry while enjoying the sandwiches. (15 minutes)

14. Chocolate Constellations:

- Ingredients: Melted chocolate, assorted candies
- Directions: Arrange candies on a chocolate canvas to represent constellations. Discuss astronomy concepts. (25 minutes)

15. Marshmallow Structures:

- Ingredients: Mini marshmallows, toothpicks
- Directions: Build structures using mini marshmallows and toothpicks, discussing stability and architecture. (30 minutes)

16. Fruit and Veggie Printing:

- Ingredients: Various fruits and vegetables, paint, paper
- Directions: Dip fruits and veggies in paint, stamp on paper, and discuss patterns and shapes. (20 minutes)

17. Edible Rainbow Science:

- **Ingredients:** Skittles, water
- **Directions:** Arrange Skittles in a circle on a plate, pour water in the center, and observe the rainbow of colors. Discuss color mixing and density. (20 minutes)

18. Holiday Ice Cream in a Bag:

- **Ingredients:** 3 cups Ice, ⅓ cup kosher salt, 2 Tablespoons sugar, ½ teaspoon vanilla extract, 1 cup milk or half-and-half for an even creamier texture
- **Directions:** Make ice cream in a bag: 1. In a small resealable bag, combine milk, sugar, and vanilla. Push out the excess air and seal. 2. In a large resealable plastic bag, combine ice and salt. Place the small bag inside the bigger bag and shake vigorously 8-10 minutes until the ice cream has hardened. 3. Remove from the bag and enjoy with your favorite toppings! 4. Discuss the freezing points. (30 minutes)

19. Jellybean STEM Structures:

- Ingredients: Jellybeans, toothpicks
- Directions: Build structures using jellybeans and toothpicks, discussing engineering concepts. (25 minutes)

20. Chocolate-Dipped Pretzel Patterns:

- Ingredients: Pretzel rods, melted chocolate, assorted sprinkles
- Directions: Dip pretzel rods in chocolate and decorate with sprinkles to create patterns. Discuss patterns in nature. (20 minutes)

21. Edible Christmas Tree Cones:

- Ingredients: Sugar cones, green icing, assorted candies
- Directions: Ice cones with green icing and decorate with candies. (15 minutes)

22. Candy Cane Science Experiment:

- Ingredients: Candy canes
- Directions: Observe how candy canes dissolve in hot and cold liquids. (10 minutes)

23. Holiday Jell-O Science:

- Ingredients: Red and green Jell-O, gummy shapes
- Directions: Make Jell-O according to package instructions, and add gummy shapes. (2 hours, including chilling time)

24. Fizzy Ornament Art:

- Ingredients: Baking soda, vinegar, food coloring
- Directions: Mix baking soda and water, shape into ornaments, drop colored vinegar for a fizzy reaction. (20 minutes)

25. Christmas Cookie Structures:

- Ingredients: Gingerbread cookies, icing
- Directions: Build structures using gingerbread cookies and icing as "glue." (30 minutes)

26. Peppermint Playdough:

- Ingredients: Flour, salt, peppermint extract, water, red food coloring
- Directions: Mix ingredients to create peppermint-scented playdough. (20 minutes)

27. Edible Snowman Craft:

- Ingredients: Marshmallows, pretzel sticks, chocolate chips
- Directions: Assemble snowmen using marshmallows, pretzels, and chocolate chips. (15 minutes)

28. Melting Snowman Cookies:

- **Ingredients:** Sugar cookies, icing, marshmallows
- **Directions:** Decorate cookies with icing and marshmallows. Make it look like the snowman is melting. Use your creative juices to create your masterpiece! (25 minutes)

29. Gingerbread House Engineering:

- **Ingredients:** Gingerbread house kit or homemade gingerbread, icing, candies
- **Directions:** Follow kit instructions or assemble homemade gingerbread houses with candies. (1 hour)

30. Cranberry Engineering Structures:

- **Ingredients:** Cranberries, toothpicks
- **Directions:** Build structures using cranberries and toothpicks. (30 minutes)

31. Chocolate Covered Pretzel Rod Trees:

- Ingredients: Pretzel rods, green candy melts, assorted decorations
- Directions: Dip pretzel rods in melted candy, decorate as Christmas trees. (20 minutes)

32. Candy Sleighs Engineering:

- Ingredients: Mini candy canes, chocolate bars, candy presents
- Directions: Attach candy canes to chocolate bars to create sleighs, add candy presents. (30 minutes)

33. Holiday Science Pop Rocks Experiment:

- Ingredients: Pop Rocks candy
- Directions: Observe the popping reaction when Pop Rocks are added to different liquids. (15 minutes)

34. Gummy Structures:

- Ingredients: Gummy candies
- Directions: Build creative structures using various shapes of gummy candies. (20 minutes)

35. Edible Snowflake Art:

- Ingredients: Pretzel sticks, white chocolate, blue sprinkles
- Directions: Arrange pretzel sticks into snowflake shapes, dip in melted chocolate, and sprinkle with blue decor. (20 minutes)

36. Candy Cane Playdough Sculptures:

- Ingredients: Candy canes, playdough
- Directions: Mold playdough into sculptures and incorporate pieces of candy canes. (15 minutes) NOTE: Do NOT eat the playdough unless it says explicitly edible playdough!

37. Jellybean Counting Math Game:

- Ingredients: Jellybeans
- Directions: Use jellybeans for counting and basic math exercises. (15 minutes)

38. Edible Marshmallow Snowflakes:

- Ingredients: Marshmallows, white chocolate, blue sprinkles
- Directions: Thread marshmallows onto pretzel sticks, dip them in melted chocolate and sprinkle them with blue decor. (20 minutes)

39. Candy Chromatography Art:

- Ingredients: Coffee filters, markers, water
- Directions: Color coffee filters with markers and dip them in water to -- chromatography art. (30 minutes). Discuss what is chromatography and the chemistry behind it. (the separation of a mixture by passing it in solution (water) through a medium (coffee filter), and the colors move at different rates.

40. Cupcake Liner Christmas Trees:

- Ingredients: Cupcake liners, glue, assorted decorations
- Directions: Fold cupcake liners into tree shapes and decorate them with various items. (20 minutes)

41. Festive Ice Cream Cone Trees:

- Ingredients: Ice cream cones, green icing, assorted sprinkles
- Directions: Ice cones with green icing, then let the kids decorate with sprinkles to create edible Christmas trees. (Time: 15 minutes)

42. Candy Cane Playdough:

- Ingredients: Peppermint extract, red food coloring, flour, salt, water
- Directions: Mix flour, salt, water, and peppermint extract to create a candy cane-scented playdough. (Time: 20 minutes)

43. Graham Cracker Gingerbread Houses:

- Ingredients: Graham crackers, royal icing, assorted candies

- Directions: Use graham crackers to build small gingerbread houses and decorate them with royal icing and candies. (Time: 30 minutes)

44. Edible Snowman Building:

- Ingredients: Marshmallows, pretzel sticks, chocolate chips, candy buttons

- Directions: Let kids use marshmallows, pretzel sticks, chocolate chips, and candy buttons to build their own edible snowmen. (Time: 20 minutes)

45. Jingle Bell Jello:

- Ingredients: Gelatin, water, jingle bells

- Directions: Make jello, add jingle bells, and let it set for a fun, jiggly sensory experience. (Time: 2 hours)

46. Cranberry Structures:

- Ingredients: Toothpicks, cranberries
- Directions: Use toothpicks and cranberries to build simple geometric structures. (Time: 15 minutes)

47. Fruit Christmas Trees:

- Ingredients: Various fruits, star-shaped cookie cutter
- Directions: Cut fruits into star shapes and let kids arrange them to make Christmas tree patterns. (Time: 15 minutes)

48. Melting Snowman Cookies:

- Ingredients: Sugar cookies, icing, marshmallows, chocolate chips
- Directions: Decorate sugar cookies to look like melting snowmen using icing, marshmallows, and chocolate chips. (Time: 25 minutes)

49. Candy Cane Science Experiment:

- Ingredients: Candy canes, various liquids (water, oil, vinegar)
- Directions: Explore solubility by placing candy canes in different liquids and observing the effects. (Time: 20 minutes)

50. Chocolate Covered Pretzel Patterns:

- Ingredients: Pretzel rods, melted chocolate, colored icing
- Directions: Dip pretzel rods in chocolate and let kids create patterns with colored icing. (Time: 25 minutes)

51. Edible Painted Ornaments:

- Ingredients: Tortillas, food coloring, edible markers, cheese
- Directions: Cut tortillas into ornament shapes, and let kids paint and decorate with edible markers and cheese. (Time: 30 minutes)

52. Pasta Sculptures:

- Ingredients: Various pasta shapes, marshmallows
- Directions: Connect pasta shapes with marshmallows to build unique sculptures. (Time: 20 minutes)

53. Fruit Kabob Engineering:

- Ingredients: Assorted fruits, skewers
- Directions: Let kids engineer their own fruit kabobs using a variety of colorful fruits. (Time: 15 minutes)

54. Gumdrop Patterns:

- Ingredients: Gumdrops, toothpicks
- Directions: Create patterns and structures using gumdrops and toothpicks. (Time: 20 minutes)

55. Edible Color Mixing:

- Ingredients: Vanilla pudding, food coloring
- Directions: Make vanilla pudding, separate into bowls, and let kids mix in different food colors. (Time: 15 minutes)

56. Christmas Cookie Tangrams:

- Ingredients: Sugar cookies, icing
- Directions: Cut sugar cookies into tangram shapes, let kids rearrange and decorate. (Time: 25 minutes)

57. Jellybean Counting:

- Ingredients: Jellybeans, numbered cups
- Directions: Use jellybeans for a counting and sorting activity by placing them into numbered cups. (Time: 15 minutes)

58. Edible Slime:

- Ingredients: Powdered sugar, marshmallows, cornstarch
- Directions: Mix powdered sugar, marshmallows, and cornstarch to create edible slime. (Time: 30 minutes)

59. Cupcake Liner Snowflakes:

- Ingredients: Cupcake liners, scissors, glue, glitter
- Directions: Fold and cut cupcake liners to create unique snowflake designs, then add glue and glitter. (Time: 20 minutes)

FUN STEAM ACTIVITIES YOU CAN EAT AGES 8-12

60. Candy Cane Catapults:

- Ingredients: Candy canes, spoons, marshmallows
- Directions: Use spoons to create catapults with candy canes, then launch marshmallows to explore physics. (Time: 20 minutes)

61. Gingerbread House Engineering:

- Ingredients: Gingerbread cookies, royal icing, assorted candies
- Directions: Build gingerbread houses, discussing architectural principles and design. (Time: 45 minutes)

62. Edible DNA Model:

- Ingredients: Licorice, colored marshmallows, toothpicks
- Directions: Create an edible DNA model using licorice as the strands and marshmallows as nucleotides. (Time: 30 minutes)

63. Marshmallow Snowman Engineering:

- Ingredients: Marshmallows, toothpicks, pretzels
- Directions: Build snowmen using marshmallows and toothpicks, discussing structural stability. (Time: 25 minutes)

64. Cookie Cutter Puzzles:

- Ingredients: Sugar cookie dough, cookie cutters
- Directions: Cut sugar cookies into puzzle shapes, then assemble and decorate. (Time: 30 minutes)

65. Edible Geodesic Domes:

- Ingredients: Gumdrops, toothpicks
- Directions: Build geodesic domes using gumdrops and toothpicks, exploring geometry. (Time: 40 minutes) Geodesic domes are hemisphere structures with triangular elements that hold them together. Think Epcot at Disney World.

66. Cranberry Science Experiment:

- Ingredients: Cranberries, water, baking soda, vinegar
- Directions: Experiment with cranberries by observing water, baking soda, and vinegar reactions. (Time: 20 minutes)

67. Fruit Battery Experiment:

- Ingredients: Various fruits (lemons, oranges), copper and zinc coins
- Directions: Explore electricity by creating a fruit battery using citrus fruits and metal coins. (Time: 30 minutes)

68. Edible Playdough Circuits:

- Ingredients: Homemade playdough, LED lights, batteries
- Directions: Create playdough circuits by adding LED lights and batteries exploring conductivity. (Time: 35 minutes)

69. Marshmallow Constellations:

- Ingredients: Marshmallows, toothpicks
- Directions: Connect marshmallows with toothpicks to create edible constellations. (Time: 25 minutes)

70. Edible Watercolor Art:

- Ingredients: Water, food coloring, white bread
- Directions: Mix food coloring with water and use it to paint on slices of bread. (Time: 20 minutes)

71. Pretzel Rod Fractions:

- Ingredients: Pretzel rods, chocolate, sprinkles
- Directions: Cut pretzel rods into different lengths to represent fractions, then dip them in chocolate and sprinkles. (Time: 30 minutes)

72. Candy Chromatography:

- Ingredients: Coffee filters, markers, water
- Directions: Explore chromatography by placing candy colors on coffee filters and adding water. (Time: 20 minutes)

73. Chocolate Mold Science:

- Ingredients: Chocolate, molds
- Directions: Discuss states of matter and phase changes while melting and molding chocolate. (Time: 25 minutes)

74. Edible Art with Vegetables:

- Ingredients: Various vegetables, hummus or dip
- Directions: Use vegetables to create edible art with hummus or dip on a plate. (Time: 30 minutes)

75. Marshmallow Tower Challenge:

- Ingredients: Marshmallows, spaghetti
- Directions: Build tall towers using marshmallows and spaghetti, testing engineering skills. (Time: 35 minutes)

76. Edible Inkblot Art:

- Ingredients: Paper, edible ink (fruit juices)
- Directions: Create inkblot art using edible inks made from different fruit juices. (Time: 25 minutes)

77. Candy Science Experiments:

- Ingredients: Various candies, water, heat source
- Directions: Conduct simple science experiments with different candies, observing reactions to water or heat. (Time: 40 minutes)

78. Edible Rainbow Sculptures:

- Ingredients: Colored fruits (strawberries, oranges, kiwi, blueberries)
- Directions: Arrange colored fruits to create edible rainbow sculptures. (Time: 25 minutes)

79. Bread Mold Experiment:

- Ingredients: Slices of bread, different conditions (moist, dry, warm, cool)
- Directions: Observe and document bread slices in various conditions to explore mold growth. (Time: 1 week, check daily)

80. Peppermint Candy Crystal Experiment:

- Ingredients: Peppermint candies, warm water, string
- Directions: Dissolve peppermint candies in warm water, then grow peppermint crystal ornaments by suspending string in the solution. (Time: 2 hours)

81. Gingerbread House Engineering:

- Ingredients: Gingerbread cookie pieces, royal icing, assorted candies
- Directions: Construct a gingerbread house using engineering principles and decorate it with candies. (Time: 2 hours)

82. Candy Cane Science:

- Ingredients: Candy canes, hot water, cold water
- Directions: Explore the effects of temperature on candy canes by placing them in hot and cold water. (Time: 15 minutes)

83. Edible Geodes:

- Ingredients: Clear gelatin, flavored drink mix, rock candy
- Directions: Create edible geodes by mixing clear gelatin with a flavored drink mix and adding rock candy crystals. (Time: 3 hours)

84. Christmas Cookie Coding:

- **Ingredients:** Sugar cookies, icing, edible markers
- **Directions:** Introduce basic coding concepts by decorating sugar cookies with edible markers to represent code. (Time: 1.5 hours)

85. Cranberry Circuit:

- **Ingredients:** Cranberries, LED lights, copper wire
- **Directions:** Build a simple circuit by connecting cranberries with copper wire and adding LED lights. (Time: 30 minutes)

86. Melting Snowman Sensory Bags:

- **Ingredients:** Ziplock bags, hair gel, googly eyes, buttons
- **Directions:** Create melting snowman sensory bags by filling bags with hair gel, googly eyes, and buttons. (Time: 20 minutes)

87. Edible Rainbow Experiments:

- Ingredients: Skittles, water, white plate
- Directions: Observe color diffusion by placing Skittles around the edge of a white plate and adding water. (Time: 15 minutes)

88. Christmas Tree Math Puzzles:

- Ingredients: Pretzel sticks, marshmallows, edible decorations
- Directions: Use pretzel sticks and marshmallows to create edible math puzzles in the shape of Christmas trees. (Time: 45 minutes)

89. Chocolate Covered Pretzel STEM Bridges:

- Ingredients: Pretzel rods, chocolate, small candies
- Directions: Explore engineering concepts by building bridges with pretzel rods and chocolate, then test their strength. (Time: 1 hour)

90. Fruit Battery Power:

- Ingredients: Various fruits, copper and zinc nails, wires
- Directions: Build a fruit battery by connecting different fruits with copper and zinc nails and observing the power generated. (Time: 30 minutes)

91. Edible Art with Popsicles:

- Ingredients: Popsicle sticks, icing, edible decorations
- Directions: Create edible art using popsicle sticks as a canvas and decorate with icing and edible decorations. (Time: 1 hour)

92. Chocolate Constellations:

- Ingredients: Chocolate-covered pretzels, edible stars
- Directions: Arrange chocolate-covered pretzels to represent constellations and add edible stars. (Time: 30 minutes)

93. Mathematical Snowflakes:

- Ingredients: Pretzel sticks, marshmallows, edible decorations
- Directions: Construct mathematical snowflakes using pretzel sticks and marshmallows, adding edible decorations for flair. (Time: 45 minutes)

94. Jellybean Architecture:

- Ingredients: Jellybeans, toothpicks
- Directions: To explore stability and design, build architectural structures using toothpicks and jellybeans. (Time: 1 hour)

95. Fizzy Gingerbread Men:

- Ingredients: Gingerbread cookie cutouts, baking soda, vinegar
- Directions: Add baking soda to gingerbread men cutouts and watch them fizz when vinegar is added. (Time: 20 minutes)

96. Edible Snow Globe Science:

- Ingredients: Gelatin, water, edible decorations
- Directions: Mix gelatin with water and add edible decorations to create edible snow globes. (Time: 2 hours)

97. Popcorn Kernels Engineering:

- Ingredients: Popcorn kernels, toothpicks
- Directions: Build structures using popcorn kernels and toothpicks, experimenting with stability. (Time: 45 minutes)

98. Candy Constellation Art:

- Ingredients: Candy stars, icing, edible decorations
- Directions: Create edible constellation art using candy stars, icing, and edible decorations. (Time: 1 hour)

99. Cookie Chemistry:

- Ingredients: Sugar cookie dough, food coloring, icing
- Directions: Explore color mixing by dividing cookie dough, adding different food colors, and creating vibrant cookies. (Time: 30 minutes)

100. Edible Snow Globe:

- Ingredients: Clear gelatin, edible decorations, small plastic figures
- Directions: Create a festive edible snow globe using gelatin and edible decorations. (Time: 2 hours)

101. Gingerbread Geometry:

- Ingredients: Gingerbread dough, ruler
- Directions: Use gingerbread dough to create geometric shapes and discuss angles and measurements. (Time: 45 minutes)

102. Molecular Marshmallow Models:

- Ingredients: Marshmallows, toothpicks
- Directions: To learn about molecular structures, build molecular models with marshmallows and toothpicks. (Time: 45 minutes)

103. Candy Cane Engineering:

- Ingredients: Candy canes, various candies
- Directions: To explore engineering concepts, build structures with candy canes and other candies. (Time: 40 minutes)

104. Crystalized Candy Canes:

- Ingredients: Candy canes, water, string
- Directions: Create crystal formations on candy canes by dissolving and recrystallizing sugar. (Time: 2 days)

105. Edible Circuitry:

- Ingredients: Playdough, LED lights, batteries
- Directions: Explore simple circuitry by creating edible circuits using playdough, LED lights, and batteries. (Time: 1 hour)

106. Chocolate Mold Art:

- Ingredients: Melted chocolate, silicone molds, edible colors
- Directions: Pour melted chocolate into molds, layering colors for artistic chocolate creations. (Time: 40 minutes)

107. Cranberry Chemistry:

- Ingredients: Cranberries, baking soda, vinegar
- Directions: Combine cranberries with baking soda and vinegar to experiment with chemical reactions. (Time: 30 minutes)

108. Peppermint Science Experiment:

- Ingredients: Peppermints, warm water, cold water
- Directions: Observe the effects of temperature on peppermints by placing them in warm and cold water. (Time: 20 minutes)

109. Sugar Crystal Science:

- Ingredients: Sugar, water, string
- Directions: Grow sugar crystals by dissolving sugar in water and letting it recrystallize on a string. (Time: 1 week)

110. Popcorn Science:

- Ingredients: Popcorn kernels, oil, salt
- Directions: Investigate the science behind popcorn popping with different cooking methods. (Time: 30 minutes)

111. Edible Geography Maps:

- Ingredients: Sugar cookie dough, icing, food coloring
- Directions: Use cookie dough to create edible maps, adding details with icing and food coloring. (Time: 1 hour)

112. Christmas Tree Light Reflections:

- Ingredients: Water, oil, food coloring
- Directions: Experiment with light reflections by creating a Christmas tree in a water and oil mixture. (Time: 40 minutes)

113. Peppermint Playdough:

- Ingredients: Flour, salt, water, peppermint extract, red food coloring
- Directions: Mix ingredients to create scented red playdough.
- Time: 25 minutes

114. Rudolph Pancakes:

- Ingredients: Pancake mix, chocolate chips, strawberries, whipped cream
- Directions: Shape pancakes into reindeer faces, use strawberries for antlers, and chocolate chips for eyes.
- Time: 30 minutes

115. Holiday Rice Krispie Treat Wreaths:

- **Ingredients:** Rice Krispie treats, green food coloring, red candies
- **Directions:** Shape treats into wreaths, add food coloring, and decorate with candies. (30 minutes)

Baking Basics for Young Bakers

Welcome to the sweet world of baking! As you embark on this delicious journey, let's dive into the essential tools, tech tips, and safety measures every budding baker should know.

ESSENTIAL TOOLS:

1. Measuring Cups and Spoons

Accurate measurements are key to successful baking. Invest in a set of measuring cups and spoons to ensure precision in your recipes.

2. Mixing Bowls

A variety of mixing bowls in different sizes will come in handy for combining ingredients seamlessly.

3. Whisk and Spatula

Whisks are perfect for blending dry ingredients, while spatulas help you fold in delicate mixtures.

4. Rolling Pin

For those delightful cookies and pie crusts, a rolling pin is a must.

5. Baking Sheets and Pans

Equip your kitchen with quality baking sheets and pans for even baking.

TECHNOLOGY AND APPS:

1. Recipe Apps

Explore baking apps for kid-friendly recipes and step-by-step instructions. It adds a fun, interactive element to the process.

2. Kitchen Timer Apps

Set reminders for baking and cooking times using timer apps to avoid burnt treats.

SAFETY FIRST:

1. Oven Safety

- 🎁 Always use oven mitts when handling hot pans or trays.
- 🎁 Teach kids the importance of preheating the oven and how to adjust temperature settings.

2. Knife Safety

- 🎁 Supervise young bakers when using knives.
- 🎁 Instruct them on proper cutting techniques to prevent accidents.

3. Hand Hygiene and Kitchen Cleanliness:

- 🎁 Emphasize the significance of washing hands before and after handling food.

🎁 Keep the kitchen clean to prevent cross-contamination.

ADDITIONAL TIPS:

1. Follow the Recipe

Baking is a science; follow recipes closely for the best results. Encourage creativity once the basics are mastered.

2. Enjoy the Process

Baking is not just about the final product; it's about having fun along the way. Taste the joy in every step!

Happy baking, little chefs! May your kitchen be filled with laughter, sweetness, and delicious memories.

3. NOTE about Nutritional Information in the Recipes:

These values are approximate and can vary based on the specific ingredients used. This peppermint bark is a sweet holiday treat, but it's important to enjoy it in moderation as part of a balanced diet.

Baking Safety Tips for Young Bakers:

🎁 Wash Your Hands:

- Before you start baking, make sure to wash your hands thoroughly with soap and water. Clean hands help keep your treats safe and delicious!

🎁 Ask for Help:

- Always have an adult or older sibling present when using the oven, stove, or any sharp tools. They can guide you and ensure everything is safe.

🎁 Read the Recipe Together:

- Sit down with an adult and read the recipe together. Understanding each step helps you know what to do and keeps everything organized.

🎁 Use Kid-Friendly Utensils:

- Choose utensils and tools that are just the right size for you. This makes it easier to handle and reduces the risk of accidents.

- **Apron Up:**
  - Put on your apron to protect your clothes. Baking can be messy and fun, but an apron keeps your clothes clean!
- **Keep Hair Tied Back:**
  - If you have long hair, tie it back before you start. This ensures that your hair won't get in the way of your baking adventure.
- **Stay Near the Oven:**
  - When something is baking in the oven, make sure to stay nearby with an adult. This way, you can check on your tasty creation without any problems.
- **Use Oven Mitts:**
  - When taking hot pans or trays out of the oven, always use oven mitts. They keep your hands safe from the heat.

🎁 **Watch Out for Hot Surfaces:**

- 🌿 Be cautious around hot stovetops and oven doors. These surfaces can get really hot, so always ask an adult for help if you need to touch them.

🎁 **No Tasting Raw Batter:**

- 🌿 While baking, resist the temptation to taste raw batter or dough, especially if it contains raw eggs. It's much safer to enjoy the finished, baked product.

🎁 **Clean as You Go:**

- 🌿 Keep your workspace tidy by cleaning up spills and putting away ingredients as you finish using them. A clean kitchen is a safe kitchen!

🎁 **Have Fun and Be Patient:**

- 🌿 Baking is a joyful experience! Take your time, enjoy the process, and remember, it's okay to ask for help if you're unsure about something.

These safety tips are designed to make baking a fun and secure activity for young chefs, ensuring a positive and delicious experience in the kitchen.

CHAPTER 4

Morning Magic:
Breakfast Bites and STEAM Delights

Chocolate Waffles

Serves 14

Notes: These are great for "W" day for Kindergarten snacks.

They taste amazing, frosted or covered with whipped cream, chocolate syrup, or fudge sauce. Sliced strawberries, raspberries, and or sliced bananas are excellent on top.

Ingredients

1 cup butter, softened
4 beaten eggs
1 ½ cups sugar
½ cup cocoa
2 cups flour
1 teaspoon vanilla extract
1 teaspoon salt
½ cup water
½ cup milk

Directions

1. Mix all ingredients in a bowl. The hand mixer works great.

2. Drop batter onto a waffle iron. Some waffle irons need Pam spray so the waffle will slip right out.

3. Bake in waffle iron for 1-3 minutes, on medium setting. (depends on your waffle maker).

Nutrition Facts (Per serving, assuming 10 servings):

- Calories: 430 kcal
- Total Fat: 25g
  - o Saturated Fat: 15g
  - o Trans Fat: 1g
- Cholesterol: 150mg
- Sodium: 370mg
- Total Carbohydrates: 50g
  - o Dietary Fiber: 2g
  - o Total Sugars: 31g
- Protein: 7g

Pumpkin Waffles

Notes: Serve with maple syrup, honey, or just with butter.

Ingredients

½ cup canned pumpkin puree
½ cup sour cream
½ cup milk
2 eggs, separated
½ cup melted butter
2 Tablespoons brown sugar (can use 3 TBSP for a sweeter waffle)
¾ cup all-purpose flour
1 teaspoon baking powder
¼ teaspoon baking soda
¼ teaspoon salt
1 teaspoon cinnamon
¼ teaspoon nutmeg

Directions

1. Heat waffle maker. Spray with Pam spray if that is how you prepare your waffle maker.

2. Whisk together pumpkin puree, sour cream, milk, 2 egg yolks, melted butter, and brown sugar in a large bowl.

3. Combine ¾ cups 2 tablespoons flour, baking powder, baking soda, salt, cinnamon and nutmeg in another bowl.

4. Add the dry ingredients to the pumpkin mixture. Mix well until combined.

5. In another bowl, beat the egg whites until stiff peaks form. Fold into the waffle mixture until combined.

6. Bake in preheated waffle iron.

7. Enjoy!

Nutrition Facts (Per serving, assuming 8 servings):

- Calories: 290 kcal
- Total Fat: 21g
  o Saturated Fat: 12g
  o Trans Fat: 1g
- Cholesterol: 105mg
- Sodium: 340mg
- Total Carbohydrates: 23g
  o Dietary Fiber: 1g
  o Total Sugars: 6g
- Protein: 5g

Christmas Crepes!

Notes: Step 1: Blend the ingredients and let sit for 1 hour.

Ingredients

2 large eggs, room temperature
1 ¼ c. whole milk, room temperature
1 c. all-purpose flour
4 tsp. granulated sugar
½ tsp. salt
3 tbsp. unsalted butter, melted, cooled, plus ½ tsp. cold unsalted butter
Fresh berries and powdered sugar for serving (optional)

Directions

1. Blend eggs, milk, flour, granulated sugar, salt, and 3 tablespoons melted butter in a blender until smooth, about 1 minute. Cover and refrigerate for at least 1 hour or up to 2 days. (Yes, this step is very important)

2. Preheat a 9" nonstick skillet over medium heat. Melt 1/2 teaspoon cold butter in a preheated pan. Reduce heat to medium-low. Briefly whisk the batter, then pour 1/4 cup into the center of the pan, lifting the pan off heat and slightly tilting in a circular motion to help the batter spread into an even circle. Cook until the top is set and the bottom is golden brown, about 45 seconds. Flip and cook on the second side until cooked through, about 45 seconds more.

- 3. Using a spatula, fold the crêpe into quarters. Transfer to a plate. Repeat with the remaining batter for about 8 crêpes.

- 4. Crepes can be served with berries and powdered sugar, Nutella, bananas and chocolate chips, whipped cream, and pretty much anything you can imagine. Have FUN!!

Christmas Crêpes! Continued

- Crepes can be made ahead! Crêpes can be made up to 3 days ahead. Be sure to let the crepes cool! You can store them in an airtight container and stack them between sheets of parchment paper, refrigerate, or freeze for up to 1 month.

How to make great crêpes.

— *Rest baby rest.* Crêpes cook up quickly, but the batter does need to rest for at least an hour before using. Don't skip this step! Resting the batter gives the flour a chance to hydrate so the crêpe will hold together and also allows the gluten in the flour to relax, which helps create a tender crêpe. The batter will keep in the fridge for up to 2 days, which means you can even make it the night before so it's ready to go in the morning.

— *The first is just practice.* Crêpes and pancakes have one rule in common: No matter how skilled you are, the first one is usually a disaster. It's a lesson in patience and fortitude. Press on, and things will quickly improve.

— *Pick the right pan.* One of the trickiest things about making crêpes is getting the batter to spread into an even, perfect circle in the pan. It's more difficult without a crepe pan, but you can achieve good results in a standard 8" or 9" nonstick pan.

— *Swirl the batter.* Pour the batter into the center of the pan with a ¼-cup measuring cup, then lift the pan off the stove and tilt it gently to encourage the batter to spread. It might take a little practice, but you'll soon get the hang of it (and any mistakes will still be delicious).

Nutrition Facts (Per serving, assuming 8 servings):

- Calories: 150 kcal
- Total Fat: 8g
  - Saturated Fat: 5g
  - Trans Fat: 0g
- Cholesterol: 75mg
- Sodium: 220mg
- Total Carbohydrates: 16g
  - Dietary Fiber: 0g
  - Total Sugars: 4g
- Protein: 4

Chocolatey Puff Cereal Bagel

Ingredients

4 Plain mini bagels
4 tablespoons plain cream cheese
½ cup chocolate puff cereal

ALSO try:
Fruity cereals, chocolate peanut butter puffs, and any other of your favorite cold cereals

Directions

1. Slice the bagels in half (have a grown-up help you use a knife).

2. Toast in the toaster

3. Smear each bagel top with ½ tablespoon cream cheese

4. Add Cereal to a bowl.

5. Dip the bagel into the cereal or sprinkle on top of the cream cheese.

ENJOY!

Nutrition Facts (Per Serving, assuming 4 servings):

- Calories: 270 kcal
- Total Fat: 10g
  - o Saturated Fat: 5g
  - o Trans Fat: 0g
- Cholesterol: 25mg
- Sodium: 450mg
- Total Carbohydrates: 37g
  - o Dietary Fiber: 2g
  - o Total Sugars: 5g
- Protein: 8g

Fruity Overnight Oats

Ingredients

½ cup rolled oats
½ cup milk (regular or a milk alternative)
¼ cup Greek yogurt
1 tablespoon honey or maple syrup
½ teaspoon vanilla extract
A handful of mixed berries (strawberries, blueberries, raspberries)
Sliced banana
Optional: Chia seeds or flaxseeds for added nutrition and texture

Directions

1. Combine Ingredients: In a jar or container, mix the rolled oats, milk, Greek yogurt, honey or maple syrup, and vanilla extract.

2. Add Fruits: Stir in a handful of mixed berries and sliced banana. Feel free to customize with your child's favorite fruits.

3. Optional Seeds: For added nutrition, sprinkle in a teaspoon of chia seeds or flaxseeds if your child enjoys them.

4. Mix Well: Stir all the ingredients together until well combined.

5. Refrigerate Overnight: Cover the jar or container and refrigerate overnight or for at least 4 hours. This allows the oats to absorb the liquid and become deliciously creamy.

Nutrition Facts (per serving):

- Calories: 320
- Total Fat: 8g
  - Saturated Fat: 2g
  - Trans Fat: 0g
- Cholesterol: 10mg
- Sodium: 60mg
- Total Carbohydrates: 56g
  - Dietary Fiber: 7g
  - Sugars: 26g
- Protein: 11g

Serve and Enjoy:

In the morning, stir the oats well and enjoy a nutritious and tasty breakfast!

Pomegranate Fruit Yogurt Parfait

Ingredients

1 cup vanilla yogurt
½ cup granola
½ cup pomegranate arils (seeds) or fruit of your choice
1 tablespoon honey
Festive sprinkles (optional)

Directions

1. Prepare Pomegranate Arils: Cut a pomegranate in half and gently tap the back with a wooden spoon to release the seeds (about 1/2 cup).

2. Assemble Yogurt Parfait: In a clear glass or bowl, layer the ingredients in the following order:

    o Start with a spoonful of vanilla yogurt at the bottom.

    o Add a layer of granola.

    o Sprinkle a portion of pomegranate arils over the granola.

    o Drizzle a little honey over the pomegranate layer.

3. Repeat Layers: Repeat the layers until you reach the top of the glass or bowl, finishing with a final drizzle of honey.

4. Top with Festive Sprinkles (Optional): For an extra festive touch, you can add a sprinkle of holiday-themed sprinkles on top.

5. Serve: Serve the pomegranate yogurt parfait immediately with a spoon.

This colorful and tasty treat celebrates the holiday season and incorporates the vibrant and nutritious pomegranate seeds. It's a delightful way for kids to enjoy a healthy and festive snack. Feel free to get creative with the layers and toppings based on your preferences!

A pomegranate is a seasonal food because it grows on trees and is usually ready to be picked and eaten during a specific time of the year, which is in the fall. During this season, the weather is just right for pomegranates to grow and become juicy and delicious. So, when you see pomegranates in the store or at the market, it's a sign that autumn has arrived, and it's the perfect time to enjoy this sweet and crunchy fruit!

Chapter 5

Cookie Creativity: STEAM-infused Christmas Delights for Young Bakers

S.T.E.A.M. Holiday Cookbook for Kids 4-12 85

Our Famous Sugar Cookies

Servings: 36 cookies

Notes: Store cookies in an airtight container.

Origin:
Sugar cookies have a sweet story! A long time ago, in Europe, people started making simple cookies with basic ingredients like sugar, flour, and butter. As these cookies traveled to different countries, each place added its own special touches, like decorations or different shapes. Sugar cookies are a tasty holiday tradition; we can have so much fun decorating and sharing them with friends and family! Our family recipe dates back many generations and is a fan favorite!

Ingredients

2 cups butter
3 cups sugar
4 eggs
4 teaspoon grated orange peel/4 drops orange oil
4 teaspoons vanilla extract
¾ cp milk
8-9 cups flour
1 teaspoon salt
2 teaspoons baking powder
2 teaspoons baking soda

Directions

1. Cream butter and sugar in a large mixing bowl.

2. Add 4 eggs Beat well.

3. Add orange peel/oil. Add the vanilla to the milk, then pour into the bowl.

4. Mix the flour, salt, baking soda, and baking powder in a separate bowl.

5. Combine the flour mixture with the butter mixture. A great test is to see if you can you roll the dough in your hands and see if it is sticky? If the dough is sticky, just add some more flour.

6. Roll the dough out on a floured surface with your rolling pin. Cut out shapes. You might have to have an adult help you transfer to the baking sheet. Silicone non-stick baking sheets are perfect, and we highly recommend them.

7. Bake the cookies for about 8 minutes. Remember, each oven bakes differently, so test the first batch so they don't burn. TIP: Cut out the same size shapes for one pan so the cookies bake evenly.

8. Frost and decorate!

Nutrition Facts (Per serving, assuming 10 servings):

- Calories: 230 kcal
- Total Fat: 11g
  - Saturated Fat: 7g
  - Trans Fat: 0g
- Cholesterol: 45mg
- Sodium: 260mg
- Total Carbohydrates: 30g
  - Dietary Fiber: 1g
  - Total Sugars: 13g
- Protein: 3g

Chocolate Chip Cookies

Origin:

A wonderful tale surrounds the chocolate chip cookie! In the 1930s, a clever woman named Ruth Wakefield was making regular cookies when she added small pieces of chocolate, hoping they would melt into the dough. Surprise! The chocolate stayed in bits, creating the first-ever chocolate chip cookie. Kids and adults loved it so much that it became a classic treat millions worldwide enjoyed. Every time we munch on a chocolate chip cookie, we remember Ruth's brilliant idea!

Ingredients

1 cup butter
¾ cup sugar
¾ cup brown sugar
1 tsp vanilla extract
1 tsp water
2 eggs
3 cups flour
1 tsp baking soda
1 tsp salt
1 package of chocolate chips

Directions

1st layer:
Mix crushed cookies with butter. Press in 9x13 pan.

2nd layer:
Mix ½ of the container of Cool Whip with softened cream cheese spread on crust.

3rd layer:
Mix instant chocolate pudding with milk. Spread on top.

4th layer:
Top with remaining Cool Whip and sprinkle with crushed Oreos.

Refrigerate
Cut in squares to serve.

Nutrition Facts (Per Serving, assuming 12 servings):

- Calories: 430 kcal
- Total Fat: 30g
  - Saturated Fat: 17g
  - Trans Fat: 0g
- Cholesterol: 60mg
- Sodium: 480mg
- Total Carbohydrates: 40g
  - Dietary Fiber: 1g
  - Total Sugars: 26g
- Protein: 5g

Reindeer Brownies

Origin:
Reindeer brownies have a magical story! A long time ago, during the holiday season, someone decided to turn regular brownies into festive reindeers to celebrate Santa's helpers. Using candy and pretzels, they transformed the brownies into cute reindeer faces. Now, every year, kids and families make these special brownies to enjoy a bit of holiday magic and deliciousness together!

Ingredients

4 ounces unsweetened chocolate
¾ cup cubed butter
3 large eggs
2 cups sugar
1 teaspoon vanilla extract
¼ teaspoon salt
1 cup all-purpose flour
1 can (16 ounces) frosting
48 candy eyeballs
24 red-hot candies
24-48 miniature pretzels

Directions

1. Preheat oven to 350°F

2. Line a 13X9 pan with foil. Leave extra on the sides. Lightly grease the foil.

3. Mix the chocolate and butter in a microwave-safe bowl; stir until smooth.

4. Mix eggs, sugar, vanilla, and salt together. Add the flour. Mix together to make the brownie batter.

5. Pour batter into the prepared 13x9 pan.

6. Bake at 350°F for 25-30 minutes, or until the sides pull away from the edge.

7. Cool completely.

8. Lift the foil and remove brownies from the pan.

9. Cut the brownies into squares. Then cut diagonally to create 2 triangles.

10. Attach candies and pretzels to make reindeer faces.

11. ENJOY!

Nutrition Facts (Per serving, assuming 10 servings):

1 brownie: 353 calories, 16g fat (8g saturated fat), 51mg cholesterol, 243mg sodium, 50g carbohydrate (37g sugars, 1g fiber), 3g protein.

Hot Chocolate Peppermint Cookies

Prep Time: 30 minutes | **Bake Time:** 10 min/batch + cooling

Baking Tips!
If you don't want to mess with the marshmallow creme mess, then don't! Just add a Hershey's® chocolate kiss on top instead! If the batter seems dry, simply add 1-2 tablespoons of water or milk to the batter.

Ingredients
- 1 cup butter, softened
- 1 cup sugar
- 1 large egg
- 1 teaspoon peppermint extract
- 2⅓ cups all-purpose flour
- ⅓ cup baking cocoa
- ½ teaspoon salt
- 1 teaspoon baking soda
- 1 package (11 ½ ounces) milk chocolate chips
- 1 cup marshmallow creme
- 1 cup peppermint candies, finely crushed

Directions
1. Preheat oven to 375°F In a large bowl, cream butter and sugar until light and fluffy. 5-7 minutes.
2. Beat in egg. Add peppermint extract.
3. Combine flour, cocoa powder, salt, and baking soda in a separate bowl.
4. Add flour mixture to the creamed butter and sugar mixture. Mix well.
5. Drop by tablespoonfuls about 2 inches apart onto a greased cookie sheet or lined with silicone baking mats.
6. Bake until tops are cracked, 10-12 minutes. Remove the cookies to a cooling rack to cool completely.
7. In a microwave-safe bowl, melt the chocolate chips. Stir until smooth. Drop a teaspoonful of marshmallow creme into the center of each cookie. Dip half of the cookie into the melted chocolate. Allow the excess chocolate to drip off. Immediately sprinkle with candies.
8. Place on waxed paper and let stand until set. Store in an airtight container.

CHAPTER 6

Cookie Creativity: STEAM-infused Christmas Delights

Gingerbread

Gingerbread has a rich history that dates back centuries. Its origins can be traced to medieval Europe, where it was initially created in the 10th century by Armenian monk Gregory of Nicopolis. He is credited with bringing gingerbread to Europe, and it gained popularity for both its unique taste and medicinal properties.

The concept of gingerbread spread across Europe, and by the late Middle Ages, it became associated with festive occasions and celebrations. In particular, it became a staple during Christmas and other holidays. The first

recorded instance of gingerbread figures, shaped and decorated like humans and animals, was in the court of Elizabeth I of England. These elaborately decorated gingerbread creations were often presented as gifts and became a symbol of hospitality.

The tradition of gingerbread houses became popular in Germany during the 16th century, especially after the publication of the Grimm Brothers' fairy tale "Hansel and Gretel," where the children encounter a house made of gingerbread and sweets in the woods.

Over time, various regions developed their own versions of gingerbread, incorporating local spices and flavors. Today, gingerbread is enjoyed worldwide, especially during the holiday season, and it comes in various forms, such as cookies, cakes, and houses, each reflecting cultural and regional influences.

Easy Gingerbread Cookies

Ingredients

3 cups all-purpose flour
1 teaspoon baking soda
¼ teaspoon salt
1 tablespoon ground ginger
1 tablespoon ground cinnamon
½ teaspoon ground cloves
½ cup unsalted butter, softened
½ cup brown sugar, packed
¼ cup molasses
1 large egg
1 teaspoon vanilla extract

Directions

1. **Preheat the Oven:** Preheat your oven to 350°F (175°C). Line baking sheets with parchment paper or the sillicone sheets.

2. **Whisk Dry Ingredients:** In a medium bowl, whisk together the flour, baking soda, salt, ginger, cinnamon, and cloves. Set aside.

3. **Cream Butter and Sugar:** In a large bowl, cream together the softened butter and brown sugar until light and fluffy.

4. **Add Wet Ingredients:** Beat in the molasses, egg, and vanilla extract until well combined.

5. **Combine Wet and Dry Ingredients:** Gradually add the dry ingredients to the wet ingredients, mixing until a soft dough forms.

6. **Chill the Dough (Optional):** If time allows, you can chill the dough in the refrigerator for about 30 minutes. This step is optional but can make the dough easier to handle.

7. **Roll and Cut Shapes:** On a floured surface, roll out the dough to about 1/4-inch thickness. Use cookie cutters to cut out your desired shapes.

Easy Gingerbread Cookies Continued

8. **Place on Baking Sheets:** Transfer the cutouts onto the prepared baking sheets, leaving some space between each cookie.

9. **Bake:** Bake in the preheated oven for 8-10 minutes or until the edges are lightly browned. Keep a close eye on them to prevent over-baking.

10. **Cool and Decorate:** Allow the cookies to cool on the baking sheets for a few minutes before transferring them to a wire rack to cool completely. Once cooled, you can decorate them with icing, sprinkles, or enjoy them as is!

Easy Breezy GINGERBREAD House Contest

Do you want a super duper easy activity? Make it into a neighborhood or friend contest?

Make gingerbread houses out of graham crackers and a tub of frosting! Grab a gift card for the winner, and the winner takes it all. Add a swimming pool? Add a deck? Add trees? Let your imagination go wild! Supplies: graham crackers, tubs of frosting, candies, sprinkles, candy bars, candy canes, and anything else you can imagine or see in the candy aisle. Ready, Set, CREATE!

Gingerbread STEAM Buns

Let's explore yeast in a STEAM yummy holiday recipe!

Ingredients

For the Dough:
2¼ teaspoons (1 packet) active dry yeast
1 cup warm milk (around 110°F or 43°C)
¼ cup granulated sugar
⅓ cup unsalted butter, melted
1 large egg
3½ cups all-purpose flour
1 teaspoon ground ginger
½ teaspoon ground cinnamon
¼ teaspoon ground nutmeg
¼ teaspoon salt

For the Filling:
⅓ cup brown sugar
•1 tablespoon ground cinnamon
½ cup raisins or chopped nuts (optional)

For the Icing:
1 cup powdered sugar
2 tablespoons milk
¼ teaspoon vanilla extract

Nutritional Information (per serving - 1 bun):

- Calories: 260
- Total Fat: 7g
  o Saturated Fat: 4g
  o Trans Fat: 0g
- Cholesterol: 30mg
- Sodium: 80mg
- Total Carbohydrates: 45g
  o Dietary Fiber: 1g
  o Sugars: 20g
- Protein: 4g

Directions

1. Activate the Yeast: In a small bowl, combine the warm milk and sugar. Sprinkle the yeast over the mixture, stir gently, and let it sit for about 5-10 minutes until it becomes frothy.

2. Prepare the Dough: In a large mixing bowl, whisk together the melted butter and egg. Add the activated yeast mixture and stir well. In a separate bowl, sift together the flour, ginger, cinnamon, nutmeg, and salt. Gradually add the dry ingredients to the wet ingredients, stirring until a dough forms.

3. Knead the Dough: Turn the dough onto a floured surface and knead for about 5-7 minutes until it becomes smooth and elastic. Place the dough in a lightly oiled bowl, cover it with a kitchen towel, and let it rise in a warm place for 1-1.5 hours or until it doubles in size.

4. Make the Filling: In a small bowl, mix together brown sugar and cinnamon. Set aside.

5. Shape the Buns: Punch down the risen dough and roll it out on a floured surface into a rectangle. Sprinkle the cinnamon-sugar mixture and raisins/nuts evenly over the dough. Roll the dough tightly from one end to the other, forming a log.

6. Cut and Arrange: Cut the log into 12 equal slices. Place the slices in a greased baking pan, leaving a little space between each.

7. Second Rise: Cover the pan with a kitchen towel and let the buns rise for another 30-45 minutes.

8. Bake: Preheat the oven to 350°F (180°C). Bake the buns for 20-25 minutes or until golden brown.

9. Prepare the Icing: In a small bowl, whisk together the powdered sugar, milk, and vanilla extract until smooth.

10. Ice the Buns: Once the buns have cooled slightly, drizzle the icing over the top.

11. Enjoy the Festive STEAM Buns: Dive into your delicious Gingerbread STEAM Buns, appreciating the science and artistry that went into creating this holiday treat!

Cinnamon Sugar Snowflake Rolls

Ingredients

2¼ teaspoons (1 packet) active dry yeast
1 cup warm milk (110°F/43°C)
¼ cup granulated sugar
⅓ cup unsalted butter, melted
1 teaspoon vanilla extract
3½ cups all-purpose flour
½ teaspoon salt
Cooking spray or extra butter for greasing

For the Filling:

½ cup unsalted butter, softened
½ cup brown sugar, packed
2 teaspoons ground cinnamon

For the Snowflake Glaze:

1 cup powdered sugar
2 tablespoons milk
½ teaspoon vanilla extract

Nutrition Information (per serving):

- Calories: 240
- Total Fat: 9g
  o Saturated Fat: 5g
  o Trans Fat: 0g
- Cholesterol: 25mg
- Sodium: 85mg
- Total Carbohydrates: 35g
  o Dietary Fiber: 1g
  o Sugars: 17g
- Protein: 3g

Directions

1. **Activate the Yeast:** In a bowl, combine the warm milk and sugar. Sprinkle the yeast over the mixture, stir gently, and let it sit for 5-10 minutes until it becomes frothy.
2. **Prepare the Dough:** Combine the melted butter, vanilla extract, activated yeast mixture, flour, and salt in a large mixing bowl. Stir until the dough comes together.
3. **Knead the Dough:** Transfer the dough to a floured surface and knead for about 5-7 minutes until it becomes smooth and elastic.
4. **First Rise:** Place the dough in a greased bowl, cover it with a damp cloth, and let it rise in a warm place for 1-1.5 hours or until it doubles in size.
5. **Roll Out the Dough:** Roll the dough into a rectangle (about 12x18 inches) on a floured surface.
6. **Add Filling:** Spread the softened butter over the rolled-out dough. Mix brown sugar and cinnamon and sprinkle it evenly over the butter.
7. **Create Snowflake Shapes:** Carefully fold the dough in half lengthwise and then in half again. Cut the dough into snowflake shapes using a sharp knife or pizza cutter.
8. **Second Rise:** Place the cut dough on a baking sheet lined with parchment paper. Cover with a cloth and let it rise for another 30-45 minutes.
9. **Bake:** Preheat the oven to 375°F (190°C). Bake the snowflake rolls for 12-15 minutes or until golden brown.
10. **Make the Glaze:** While the rolls are baking, whisk together powdered sugar, milk, and vanilla extract to create the glaze.
11. **Glaze the Snowflakes:** Once the rolls are out of the oven, drizzle the glaze over the warm snowflake rolls.
12. **Serve and Enjoy:** Allow the rolls to cool slightly before serving. Enjoy your delicious and festive Cinnamon Sugar Snowflake Rolls!

Festive STEAM Cinnamon Rolls

Ingredients

For the Dough:

1 cup warm milk (about 110°F)
2¼ teaspoons (1 packet) active dry yeast
¼ cup granulated sugar
⅓ cup unsalted butter, melted
1 teaspoon vanilla extract
1 teaspoon salt
3 cups all-purpose flour

For the Filling:

½ cup brown sugar, packed
2 tablespoons ground cinnamon
¼ cup unsalted butter, softened

For the Icing:

1 cup powdered sugar
2 tablespoons milk
½ teaspoon vanilla extract

Nutritional Information (per serving – 1 roll):

- Calories: 250
- Total Fat: 8g
  - Saturated Fat: 5g
  - Trans Fat: 0g
- Cholesterol: 20mg
- Sodium: 180mg
- Total Carbohydrates: 40g
  - Dietary Fiber: 1g
  - Sugars: 20g
- Protein: 4g

Directions

1. **Activate the Yeast:** In a small bowl, combine warm milk and yeast. Let it sit for 5-7 minutes until it becomes frothy.

2. **Prepare the Dough:** In a large mixing bowl, combine the activated yeast mixture, sugar, melted butter, vanilla extract, salt, and 2 cups of flour. Mix until well combined. Gradually add the remaining flour, stirring until the dough forms a soft and slightly sticky ball.

3. **Knead the Dough:** Flour a clean surface and knead the dough for about 5 minutes until it becomes smooth and elastic.

4. **First Rise:** Place the dough in a lightly greased bowl, cover it with a clean kitchen towel, and let it rise in a warm place for 1-1.5 hours or until it doubles in size.

5. **Prepare the Filling:** Mix brown sugar and ground cinnamon for the filling in a small bowl.

6. **Roll and Fill:** Preheat the oven to 350°F (175°C). Roll out the dough into a rectangle on a floured surface. Spread softened butter over the dough and sprinkle the cinnamon-sugar mixture evenly.

7. **Roll into Logs:** Roll the dough tightly into a log and cut it into 12 equal slices.

8. **Second Rise:** Place the slices in a greased baking dish, leaving space between each. Cover and let them rise for another 30 minutes.

9. **Bake:** Bake for 20-25 minutes or until the rolls are golden brown.

10. **Make the Icing:** While the rolls are cooling, whisk together powdered sugar, milk, and vanilla extract to make the icing.

11. **Ice the Rolls:** Once the rolls are cool, drizzle the icing over the top.

Easy Homemade Soft Pretzels

Ingredients

1 ½ cups warm water
1 tablespoon sugar
2 teaspoons kosher salt
1 package (2 ¼ teaspoons) active dry yeast
4 ½ cups all-purpose flour
4 tablespoons unsalted butter, melted
Cooking spray or oil, for greasing

For the Baking Soda Bath:
10 cups water
⅔ cup baking soda

Topping:
Coarse salt, to taste

Nutrition Facts (Per Serving, assuming 8 servings):

- Calories: 280
- Total Fat: 6g
  - Saturated Fat: 3g
  - Trans Fat: 0g
- Cholesterol: 15mg
- Sodium: 900mg
- Total Carbohydrates: 48g
  - Dietary Fiber: 2g
  - Sugars: 1g
- Protein: 7g

Directions

1. **Activate the Yeast:** In a bowl, combine warm water, sugar, and kosher salt. Sprinkle the yeast over the water and let it sit for about 5 minutes, until it becomes foamy.
2. **Mix the Dough:** In a large mixing bowl, combine the flour and melted butter. Pour in the yeast mixture and mix until the dough comes together. Knead the dough on a floured surface until it becomes smooth.
3. **Rise and Rest:** Place the dough in a greased bowl, cover it with a damp cloth, and let it rise in a warm place for about 1 hour or until it doubles in size.
4. **Preheat and Shape:** Preheat your oven to 450°F (230°C). Bring the water and baking soda to a boil in a large pot. Meanwhile, punch down the risen dough and divide it into 8 equal portions. Roll each portion into a rope and shape it into a pretzel.
5. **Baking Soda Bath:** Place each pretzel into the boiling baking soda water for about 30 seconds, then transfer them to a parchment-lined baking sheet.
6. **Bake:** Sprinkle the pretzels with coarse salt and bake in the preheated oven for 12-15 minutes or until golden brown.
7. **Enjoy:** Allow the pretzels to cool slightly before serving. They're best enjoyed warm!

Peppermint Bark

Ingredients

12 ounces (about 2 cups) white chocolate, chopped

12 ounces (about 2 cups) dark chocolate, chopped

1 teaspoon peppermint extract

Crushed candy canes or peppermint candies for topping

Nutrition Facts (per serving - approx. 1 ounce):

- Calories: 130
- Total Fat: 8g
  - o Saturated Fat: 5g
  - o Trans Fat: 0g
- Cholesterol: 4mg
- Sodium: 8mg
- Total Carbohydrates: 16g
  - o Dietary Fiber: 0.5g
  - o Sugars: 15g
- Protein: 1g

Directions

1. **Prepare Baking Sheet:** Line a baking sheet with parchment paper.
2. **Melt White Chocolate:** In a microwave-safe bowl, melt the white chocolate in 30-second intervals, stirring in between until smooth. Stir in half a teaspoon of peppermint extract.
3. **Spread White Chocolate:** Pour and spread the melted white chocolate evenly onto the prepared baking sheet.
4. **Chill:** Place the baking sheet in the refrigerator to allow the white chocolate to set, usually for about 15-20 minutes.
5. **Melt Dark Chocolate:** In another microwave-safe bowl, melt the dark chocolate in 30-second intervals, stirring until smooth. Stir in the remaining half teaspoon of peppermint extract.
6. **Layer Dark Chocolate:** Pour the melted dark chocolate over the set white chocolate layer.
7. **Sprinkle with Crushed Peppermint:** Quickly sprinkle crushed candy canes or peppermint candies over the dark chocolate layer before it sets.
8. **Chill Again:** Place the baking sheet back in the refrigerator to allow the entire peppermint bark to set completely, usually for about 1-2 hours.
9. **Break into Pieces:** Once set, break the peppermint bark into small, irregular pieces.

Peppermint Hot Chocolate:

- A warm and comforting drink, peppermint hot chocolate is often adorned with whipped cream and crushed candy canes, making it a delightful treat during the winter season.

Candy Cane Brownies:

- Brownies with a swirl of peppermint candy cane make for a delicious and visually appealing holiday treat. Kids love the combination of chocolate and mint flavors.

Holiday Rice Krispie Treats:

- Rice Krispie treats get a festive makeover during the holidays with the addition of red and green food coloring, and sometimes shaped into fun holiday forms like wreaths or ornaments.

Snowman Cupcakes:

- Cupcakes decorated to resemble snowmen with frosting, candy, and pretzels capture the holiday spirit. Kids enjoy both making and eating these adorable and tasty treats.

Holiday Rice Krispie Treats

Ingredients

6 cups Rice Krispies cereal

4 cups miniature marshmallows

¼ cup unsalted butter

Red and green food coloring (optional)

Holiday-themed sprinkles (optional)

Nutrition Facts (per serving - approx. 1 square):

- Calories: 90
- Total Fat: 2g
  - Saturated Fat: 1.5g
  - Trans Fat: 0g
- Cholesterol: 5mg
- Sodium: 70mg
- Total Carbohydrates: 18g
  - Dietary Fiber: 0g
  - Sugars: 8g
- Protein: 1g

Directions

1. **Prepare Baking Dish:** Grease a 9x13-inch baking dish or line it with parchment paper.

2. **Melt Marshmallows and Butter:** In a large pot, melt the butter over low heat. Add the marshmallows and stir until completely melted. If desired, add a few drops of food coloring to the marshmallow mixture for a festive touch.

3. **Combine with Rice Krispies:** Remove the pot from heat and gently fold in the Rice Krispies cereal until evenly coated with the marshmallow mixture.

4. **Press into Baking Dish:** Transfer the mixture into the prepared baking dish. Use a spatula or wax paper to press it down evenly.

5. **Add Sprinkles (Optional):** If desired, sprinkle holiday-themed sprinkles over the top of the Rice Krispie mixture and gently press them down.

6. **Allow to Set:** Let the treats cool and set for about 30 minutes before cutting them into squares or fun holiday shapes.

Snowman Cupcakes

The origin of cupcakes generally can be traced back to the 19th century, becoming more popular in the early 20th century.

Ingredients

1 box of your favorite cupcake mix (and the required ingredients listed on the box)

White frosting

Miniature marshmallows

Mini chocolate chips or chocolate-covered sunflower seeds

Orange candy-coated chocolates or orange fondant for the snowman's nose

Holiday-themed cupcake liners (optional)

Nutritional Information (per cupcake):

- Calories: 180
- Total Fat: 8g
    o Saturated Fat: 2g
    o Trans Fat: 1g
- Cholesterol: 15mg
- Sodium: 190mg
- Total Carbohydrates: 25g
    o Dietary Fiber: 0g
    o Sugars: 15g
- Protein: 2g

Directions

1. **Bake Cupcakes:** Prepare the cupcake batter according to the instructions on the box. Bake the cupcakes in festive cupcake liners if desired.

2. **Cool Cupcakes:** Allow the cupcakes to cool completely before decorating.

3. **Frost Cupcakes:** Frost the cupcakes with white frosting, creating a smooth surface.

4. **Create Snowman Face:** Place two miniature marshmallows near the top of the cupcake for the snowman's eyes. Add a chocolate chip or chocolate-covered sunflower seed in the center of each marshmallow for the eyes. Place an orange candy-coated chocolate or a small piece of orange fondant below the eyes for the snowman's nose.

5. **Form Snowman Body:** Use additional miniature marshmallows to create the snowman's body, stacking them in a line or a gentle curve down the center of the cupcake.

6. **Decorate with Buttons (Optional):** If desired, use additional miniature marshmallows or small candies to create buttons down the snowman's body.

Enjoy: Serve and enjoy these adorable Snowman Cupcakes!

Candy Cane Brownies

Brownies have a rich history and are believed to have originated in the United States during the 20th century.

Ingredients

1 box of your favorite brownie mix (ours is Ghiradelli®) (and the required ingredients listed on the box)

Crushed candy canes or peppermint candies

White chocolate chips (optional)

Peppermint extract (optional, for added flavor)

Nutritional Information (per brownie):

- Calories: 150
- Total Fat: 7g
  o Saturated Fat: 3.5g
  o Trans Fat: 0g
- Cholesterol: 15mg
- Sodium: 80mg
- Total Carbohydrates: 21g
  o Dietary Fiber: 0g
  o Sugars: 14g
- Protein: 1g

Directions

1. **Preheat Oven:** Preheat your oven according to the instructions on the brownie mix box.

2. **Prepare Brownie Batter:** Prepare the brownie batter according to the instructions on the box. If desired, add a few drops of peppermint extract to the batter for a minty flavor.

3. **Bake Brownies:** Pour the brownie batter into a greased baking pan and bake according to the instructions on the box.

4. **Cool Brownies:** Allow the brownies to cool completely once they are done baking.

5. **Top with Crushed Candy Canes:** Sprinkle a generous amount of crushed candy canes or peppermint candies over the top of the cooled brownies.

6. **Optional:** Add White Chocolate Chips: If desired, sprinkle white chocolate chips over the crushed candy canes for an extra layer of sweetness.

7. **Chill and Cut:** Place the brownies in the refrigerator for about 30 minutes to allow them to set. Once set, cut them into squares.

8. **Serve and Enjoy:** Serve these festive Candy Cane Brownies and enjoy the delightful combination of chocolate and peppermint!

Peppermint Hot Chocolate BAR

Imagine a magical Hot Chocolate Bar, like a special place just for you to make the yummiest hot chocolate ever! It's like a little party for your taste buds. Here's how you can create your own hot chocolate adventure:

Ingredients

Hot Chocolate Mix or Cocoa Powder

Milk (regular, almond, or any milk you like!)

Whipped Cream

Mini Marshmallows

Chocolate Chips

Candy Canes (crushed or whole)

Caramel Sauce

Sprinkles

Directions

1. **Make Your Hot Chocolate:** Start with a warm cup of milk. Add hot chocolate mix or cocoa powder and stir it up until it's all mixed and chocolatey.

2. **Add Toppings:** This is the fun part! Choose your favorite toppings like whipped cream clouds, mini marshmallow snow, chocolate chip mountains, and sprinkle stars.

3. **Swirl in Some Sweetness:** Drizzle caramel sauce on top for a caramel river, or crush a candy cane to make it minty fresh!

4. **Create Your Masterpiece:** Now, it's time to create your own special hot chocolate masterpiece. Pile on the toppings as high as you want!

5. **Enjoy the Magic:** Sip your hot chocolate and let the warm, chocolatey magic fill you up. It's like a cozy hug for your taste buds!

Origin Story of Hot Chocolate:

A long, long time ago, in lands far away, people discovered the joy of hot chocolate. It all began with ancient civilizations like the Aztecs in Mexico, who enjoyed a special drink made from cocoa beans. The recipe traveled through time and places, and eventually, European explorers brought it back to their homelands.

In the 17th century, hot chocolate became a royal treat in Europe. It was sipped in fancy cups by kings and queens. Over time, people started adding sugar and milk to make it even more delightful.

Now, hot chocolate is enjoyed by kids and grown-ups all around the world, especially during chilly days and magical moments. And guess what? You can create your own magic with a Hot Chocolate Bar right at home! It's like making history deliciously fun!

CHAPTER 7

Swift Sweets: Speedy STEAM Treats to Sparkle Up Your Holidays

1. Christmas Tree Pretzels:

- 🎄 Dip pretzel rods into melted green candy melts. Decorate with festive sprinkles as ornaments. Voila! Edible Christmas trees.

2. Santa Hat Brownie Bites:

- 🎄 Top mini brownie bites with a dollop of whipped cream and half of a strawberry to create adorable Santa hat treats.

3. Snowman Cheese Sticks:

- 🎄 Turn string cheese into snowmen by adding small pieces of black olives for the eyes, a tiny carrot for the nose, and a small piece of string cheese for the hat.

4. Rudolph Rice Krispie Treats:

- 🎄 Shape Rice Krispie treats into ovals, and add pretzel antlers, candy eyes, and a red M&M for Rudolph's nose. Easy and cute!

5. Reindeer Popcorn Bags:

- 🎄 Fill small clear bags with popcorn. Add googly eyes, red pom-poms for noses, and pipe cleaner antlers to turn them into festive reindeer treats.

6. Candy Cane Marshmallow Pops:

- 🎄 Skewer marshmallows onto candy canes, dip them in melted chocolate and sprinkle them with crushed candy canes. A sweet and simple holiday treat!

7. Fruit Christmas Tree:

- 🎄 Arrange green grapes in the shape of a Christmas tree on a plate. Use strawberries or other colorful fruits as ornaments.

8. Holiday Popcorn Mix:

- 🎄 Toss popcorn with melted white chocolate, holiday-colored M&M's, and pretzels for a sweet and salty treat.

These quick and easy holiday treats are not only delicious but also perfect for getting into the festive spirit with the little ones!

Jell-O Jigglers

Prep: 10 minutes   Total: 3 hours, 10 minutes (includes refrigeration)

Ingredients

2 cups boiling water (do not add cold water)

3 packages (4 serving size each) Jell-O brand gelatin, any flavor (red and green are perfect holiday colors)

Directions

Stir boiling water into the dry gelatin mix in a large bowl for at least 3 minutes. Make sure the gelatin is completely dissolved. Pour into 13x9 inch pan

Refrigerate for at least 3 hours until firm.

To Serve:

Dip the bottom of the pan in warm water for about 15 seconds.

   Cut into 24 decorative shapes

      Use cookie cutters to cut shapes out.

   Serving Idea:

Make a red pan and a green pan of Jell-o and decorate a plate to give away.

Nutrition Facts (Per serving, assuming 10 servings):

- Calories: 20 kcal
- Total Fat: 0g
  - o Saturated Fat: 0g
  - o Trans Fat: 0g
- Cholesterol: 0mg
- Sodium: 10mg
- Total Carbohydrates: 0g
  - o Dietary Fiber: 0g
  - o Total Sugars: 0g
- Protein: 1g

Taffy

Ingredients
2 cups sugar
¼ cup vinegar
¾ cup water

Directions
1. Combine all ingredients into a pot on the stove.
2. Bring to a Boil to the hardball stage on a candy thermometer.
3. Remove from heat.
4. Cool.
5. Add vanilla extract. (about 2 teaspoons)
6. PULL. And PULL. And PULL.

Nutrition Facts
(Approximate values per serving, assuming 20 servings):

- Calories: 60 kcal
- Total Fat: 0g
  o Saturated Fat: 0g
  o Trans Fat: 0g
- Cholesterol: 0mg
- Sodium: 0mg
- Total Carbohydrates: 16g
  o Dietary Fiber: 0g
  o Total Sugars: 16g
- Protein: 0g

Fantastic job on making homemade taffy! Now, let's dive into the STEAM realm with a thoughtful question:

STEAM Question:

As you stretched and pulled the taffy, did you notice any changes in its texture or appearance? How might the principles of elasticity and molecular structure explain the transformation that occurred during the taffy-making process? Consider the role of heat, sugar crystallization, and the physical manipulation of the candy in your response.

This question encourages reflection on the scientific principles involved in the taffy-making process, such as how heat affects molecular structures, how sugar crystals form, and how the physical action of stretching impacts the candy's texture. Happy exploring!

Caramel Popcorn

Ingredients
1 cup white Karo syrup
½ cup butter
2 cups (1 lb) brown sugar
1 can Eagle Brand milk
1-2 cups of popped popcorn

Directions
1. Combine all ingredients in a pot on the stove.
2. Boil all ingredients together to the softball stage on a candy thermometer.
3. Pour over a pan of popcorn.

Nutrition Facts
(Approximate values per serving, assuming 10 servings):

- Calories: 300 kcal
- Total Fat: 12g
  o Saturated Fat: 7g
  o Trans Fat: 0g
- Cholesterol: 35mg
- Sodium: 85mg
- Total Carbohydrates: 48g
  o Dietary Fiber: 0g
  o Total Sugars: 47g
- Protein: 1g

CHAPTER 8

Conversions & Equivalents

The recipes in this book were created using standard U.S. measurements.

The charts below offer equivalents for U.S. and Metric conversions.

NOTE: All conversions are approximate and rounded to the nearest whole number.

These equivalents will help young chefs understand and apply different measurements while having a blast with our holiday STEAM cookbook!

1 cup of Flour = 16 tablespoons
1 cup of Sugar = 48 teaspoons
1 cup of Butter = 2 sticks or 16 tablespoons
1 cup of Chocolate Chips = 6 ounces
1 cup of Milk = 240 milliliters
1 cup of Heavy Cream = 240 milliliters
1 cup of Honey = 340 grams
1 cup of Nuts = 4.5 ounces

1 Tablespoon = 3 teaspoons

Volume Equivalents:

- 1 teaspoon (tsp) = 5 milliliters (ml)
- 1 tablespoon (tbsp) = 15 milliliters (ml)
- 1 fluid ounce (fl oz) = 30 milliliters (ml)
- 1 cup = 240 milliliters (ml)
- 1 pint (pt) = 480 milliliters (ml) = 2 cups
- 1 quart (qt) = 960 milliliters (ml) = 4 cups
- 1 gallon (gal) = 3,840 milliliters (ml) = 16 cups

Weight Equivalents:

- 1 ounce (oz) = 28 grams (g)
- 1 pound (lb) = 16 ounces (oz) = 454 grams (g)

Temperature Equivalents:

- 350°F = 180°C
- 375°F = 190°C
- 400°F = 200°C
- 425°F = 220°C
- 450°F = 230°C

CHAPTER 9

BONUS!
Holiday Dad Jokes

Hello, little bakers and families! We are excited to welcome you to our Kids Holiday STEAM cookbook's festive and fun-filled "Holiday Dad Jokes" section.

Holidays are all about joy, laughter, and creating special memories together. In this section, get ready for a sprinkle of giggles and a dash of cheesy humor with a collection of delightful dad jokes that'll have the whole family in stitches. These jokes are a treat for your taste buds and a recipe for laughter, making your holiday cooking experience extra special.

As you flip through the pages and whip up delicious holiday treats, share these dad jokes with your family and friends.

After all, a good laugh is the secret ingredient that makes every dish taste even better!

So, tie on those aprons, gather around the kitchen, and let's add a pinch of humor to our holiday celebrations. Get ready for a belly full of laughs and a table full of tasty creations!

Feel free to share your favorite jokes and creations on social media! Tag @ajkikumoto, and let's spread the joy and laughter this holiday season. Get ready to roll your eyes and roll out some delicious holiday memories! #HolidayDadJokes

1. What do Santa's little helpers learn at school?
The elf-abet.

2. Where does santa keep all his money?
At the snow bank.

3. What do you get when you cross a snowman with a vampire?

Frostbite.

4. What do santa's elves drive?

Mini vans

5. What does the gingerbread man put on his bed?

Cookie sheets.

6. What do snowmen call their offspring?

Chill-dren.

7. How much did Santa pay for his sleigh?

Nothing. It was on the house.

8. What do you call a snowman with a six-pack?

An abdominal snowman.

9. What did one snowman say to the other?

Do you smell carrots?

10. What is the best Christmas present?

A broken drum, you just can't beat it.

11. What are the best Christmas sweaters made from?

Fleece Navidad.

12. What does Santa suffer from if he gets stuck in a chimney?

Claustrophobia.

13. What do reindeers say before they tell you a joke?

This one's gonna sleigh you!

14. What do you call a bankrupt Santa?

Saint Nickel-less.

15. Why do Christmas trees like the past so much?

Because the present's beneath them.

16. Where do Santa's reindeer stop for coffee?

Star-bucks.

17. What's every elf's favorite type of music?

Wrap.

18. Why does Santa always enter through the chimney?

Because it soots him.

19. What do you call a snowman that can walk?

Snow-mobile.

20. What is Santa's favorite place to deliver presents?

Idaho-ho-ho.

21. What's the difference between the Christmas alphabet and the ordinary alphabet?

The Christmas alphabet has No-el.

22. What do reindeer hang on their Christmas trees?

Hornaments.

23. Why didn't Rudolph go to school?

He was elf-taught.

24. Who is Santa's favorite singer?

Elf-is Presley.

25. What do elves post on Social Media?

Elf-ies.

26. What kind of motorbike does Santa ride?

A Holly Davidson!

27. Did you hear that Santa knows karate?
He has a black belt.

28. Who delivers Christmas presents to sharks?
Santa Jaws.

29. Which of Santa's reindeer has bad manners?
Rude-olph.

30. What's Santa Claus's favorite type of potato chip?
Crisp Pringles.

31. How did Scrooge win the football game?
The ghost of Christmas passed.

32. Why are Christmas trees so bad at sewing?
They always drop their needles.

33. What did the beaver say to the Christmas Tree?
Nice gnawing you.

34. Why does Santa have three gardens?
So he can ho ho ho.

35. What do you get if Santa goes down the chimney when a fire is lit?

Krisp Kringle.

36. What says Oh Oh Oh?

Santa walking backward.

37. What is Santa's nationality?

He's North Pole-ish

38. How does Santa take photos?

With a Pole-aroid camera, of course.

39. What does Santa eat for breakfast?

Frosted Flakes

40. Where does Santa store his suit?

In his Clause-et.

41. Why do snowmen live at the North Pole?

Because it's cool.

42. Why shouldn't you trust snowmen?

They're always up to snow good.

43. What did the ocean say when Santa flew over?

Nothing. It just waved.

44. Why does The Grinch enjoy gardening?

He's got a green thumb.

45. What's a sheep's favorite Christmas song?

Fleece Navidad.

46. Where do you go to find reindeer?

It depends on where you left them.

47. What did one angel say to the other?

Halo there!

48. Do snow globes ever get scared?

No, just shaken.

49. What did one Christmas tree say to the other?

You need to lighten up.

50. Which of Santa's reindeer has the best moves?

Dancer.

50. Did you hear about the angry snowman?

It had a meltdown.

51. Who's the snowman's favorite rapper?

Ice Cube.

52. Where do gingerbread men sleep?

On cookie sheets.

53. What did Santa and Mrs. Claus name their daughter?

Mary Christmas.

54. Where does Santa stay on vacation?

At a ho-ho-ho-tel.

55. What do you call festive ducks?

Christmas quackers.

56. What did one snowman say to the other?

You're cool.

57. What do you call a snowman with no arms or legs?

A snowball.

58. Knock, knock! Who's there? Snow. Snow who?

Snow one's better than you are!

59. Knock, knock! Who's there? Sandy. Sandy who?

Sandy Claus is coming to town.

60. Knock, knock! Who's there? Mary. Mary who?

Mary Christmas.

61. Knock, knock! Who's there? Tree. Tree who?

Tree wise men.

62. Knock, knock! Who's there? Donut. Donut who?

Donut open the presents until Christmas.

63. Knock, knock! Who's there? Arthur. Arthur who?

Arthur any more presents?

64. Knock, knock! Who's there? Santa. Santa who?

Santa Claus, duh!

65. Knock, knock! Who's there? Yule. Yule who?

Yule never know.

66. Knock, knock! Who's there? Water. Water who?

Water you askin' Santa for Christmas?

67. Why is it always cold on Christmas?

Because it's in Decem-burr.

68. What did Santa say after returning to the North Pole?

There's snow place like home.

69. Why did the snowman get in trouble?

He was up to snow good.

70. What do elves do after school?

Their gnome work.

71. What kind of ball doesn't bounce?

A snow ball.

72. I come in many colors, so beautiful and bright, I turn so many houses into a beautiful sight. What am I?

Christmas Lights

73. What do you get when you cross a Christmas tree with an apple?

A pineapple

74. Why did the gingerbread man go to the doctor during the holidays?

Because he was feeling a bit crumby!

75. What do you call an elf who tells jokes?

A "punch"-line elf!

76. Why did the snowman bring a broom to the holiday party?

Because he wanted to sweep the season!

77. How does a snowman get around?

By riding an "icicle"

78. Why did the Christmas tree go to the barber?

It needed a trim!

79. What did one ornament say to the other?

"I like hanging out with you!"

80. Why did Santa's helper see the doctor?

Because he had low "elf" esteem!

81. What did one snowman say to the other?

"Do you smell carrots?"

82. What did the gingerbread man use to fix his house?

Icing and gumdrops!

Chapter 10

STEAM Challenge Planner
STEAM Exploration
Fraction Chart
Math: Double That Recipe!
My Recipe Template

Welcome to the heart of our Holiday STEAM Cookbook, where the kitchen becomes a canvas for creativity, learning, and a dash of holiday magic! We are thrilled to guide you through the exciting resources and worksheets we designed for Zoey's Great Adventures™ Learns to Bake: A S.T.E.A.M. Holiday Cookbook for Kids 4-12. Be prepared to elevate your culinary experience to a new level.

Get ready to turn your kitchen into a laboratory of learning and fun!

1. **STEAM Challenge Planner**

Embark on a culinary adventure with our STEAM Challenge Planner. Plan your baking projects like a true STEAM explorer. From listing materials to predicting outcomes, this planner is your roadmap to a hands-on, educational baking experience. Prepare for a dash of science, a pinch of technology, a sprinkle of engineering, a splash of art, and a measure of mathematics!

2. **STEAM Exploration Worksheet**

Dive deep into the science behind your favorite holiday recipes with our STEAM Exploration Worksheet. Investigate the chemical reactions, explore the physics of baking, and uncover the mathematical patterns in your culinary creations. This worksheet is your passport to a world where baking and learning go hand in hand.

3.   Double that Recipe!

Have you ever wondered about the science behind doubling a recipe? Learn about the science of proportions, explore the art of flavor combinations, and discover the mathematical precision behind doubling, tripling, quadrupling or even halving those delicious ingredients. It's not just about the taste but the STEAM-powered journey in the kitchen.

4.   My Recipe: Create Your Own Recipe

Calling all young culinary inventors! Unleash your creativity with the "Create Your Own Recipe" worksheet. The Create Your Own Recipe worksheet is your blank canvas. Design a dish representing your holiday spirit and experiment with flavors, textures, and colors to create a masterpiece. It's not just a recipe – it's your masterpiece, combining the art of baking and the science of flavor.

So, grab your aprons and chef hats, sharpen your pencils, and let the holiday STEAM adventures begin! We're not just baking; we're exploring, experimenting, and savoring the joy of learning. Happy baking, little chefs! 🌟👱‍♀️🔍🔍

#HolidaySTEAMcookbook

Name _____ Date _____

STEAM CHALLENGE PLANNING DOCUMENT

Imagine: What are your ideas for the challenge?

Design: Draw and label your design. Create it.

Test:
Did your design work?
Yes. ☐   No. ☐

Improve: What changes can you make to your design to improve it?

Reflect: Talk to your partner. What did you learn from the activity? What did or didn't work?

Chef Name _____   **Date** _____

STEAM EXPLORATION
A worksheet to record your data.

Today I am exploring:

My supplies:

Steps I will take:

1.
2.
3.
4.
5.
6.

Fraction Chart

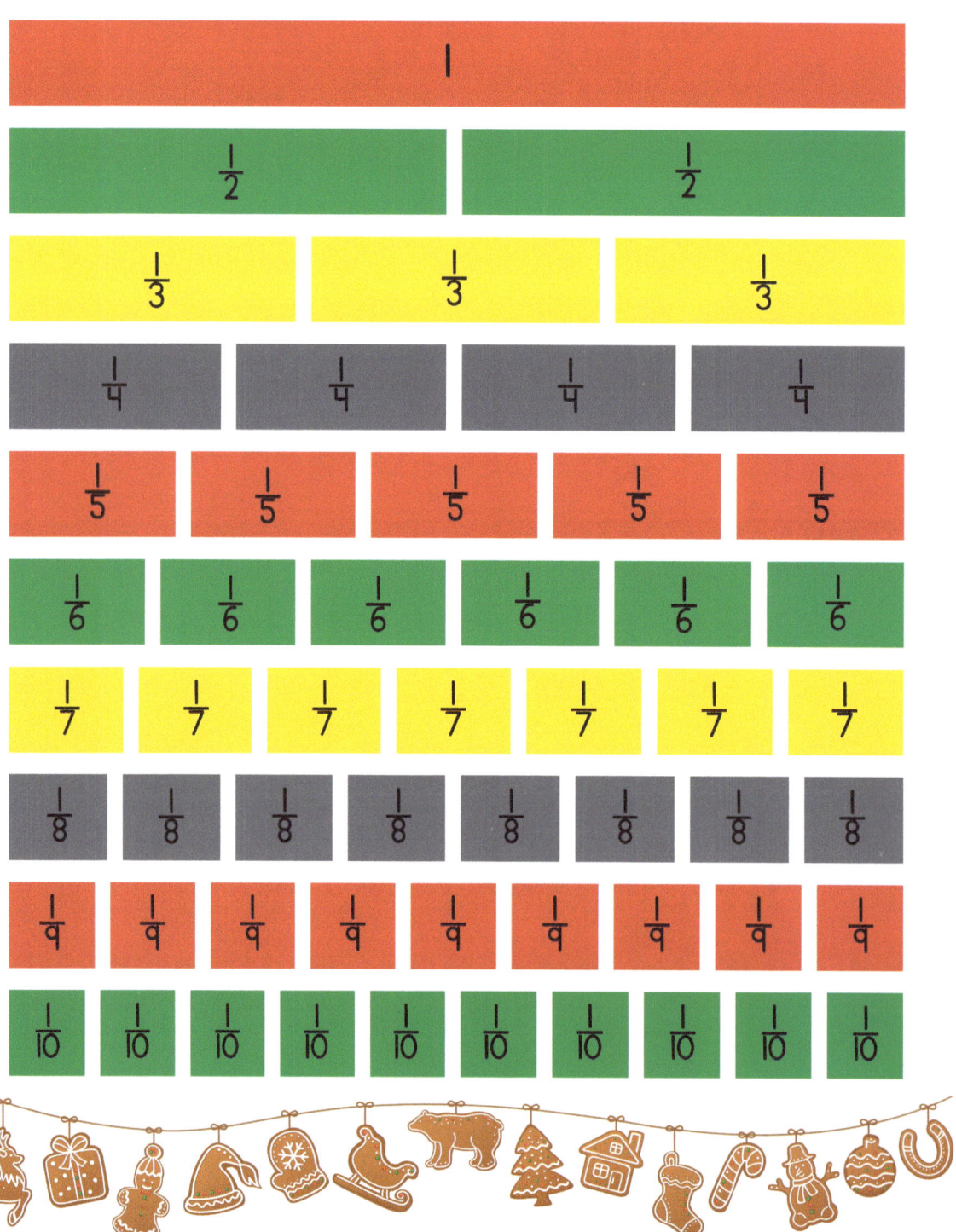

Math
Double that Recipe!

Serves 14	Double (X2)	Triple (X3)	Quadruple (X4)
Ingredients			
1 cup butter, softened			
4 beaten eggs			
1 ½ cups sugar			
½ cup cocoa			
2 cups flour			
1 teaspoon vanilla extract			
1 teaspoon salt			
½ cup water			
½ cup milk			

Serves 14	Half (/2)	1/4 (/4)
Ingredients		
1 cup butter, softened		
4 beaten eggs		
1 ½ cups sugar		
½ cup cocoa		
2 cups flour		
1 teaspoon vanilla extract		
1 teaspoon salt		
½ cup water		
½ cup milk		

Name that Recipe! _____

(HINT: breakfast recipe)

ANSWER KEY
Math
Double that Recipe!

Serves 14	Double (X2) 28	Triple (X3) 42	Quadruple (X4) 56
Ingredients			
1 cup butter, softened	2 cups	3 cups	4 cups
4 beaten eggs	8 eggs	12 eggs	16 eggs
1 ½ cups sugar	3 cups	4 1/2 cups	6 cups
½ cup cocoa	1 cup	1 1/2 cups	2 cups
2 cups flour	4 cups	6 cups	8 cups
1 teaspoon vanilla extract	2 tsp	3 tsp (1 TB)	4 tsp (1 TB 1 tsp)
1 teaspoon salt	2 tsp	3 tsp (1 TB)	4 tsp (1 TB 1 tsp)
½ cup water	1 cup	1 1/2 cups	2 cups
½ cup milk	1 cup	1 1/2 cups	2 cups

Serves 14	Half (/2) 7	1/4 (/4) 3 1/2
Ingredients		
1 cup butter, softened	1/2 cup	1/4 cup
4 beaten eggs	2 eggs	1 egg
1 ½ cups sugar	3/4 cup	1/4 cup + 2 TB or 6 TB
½ cup cocoa	1/4 cup	1/8 cup or 2 TB
2 cups flour	1 cup	1/2 cup
1 teaspoon vanilla extract	1/2 tsp	1/4 tsp
1 teaspoon salt	1/2 tsp	1/4 tsp
½ cup water	1/4 cup	1/8 cup or 2 TB
½ cup milk	1/4 cup	1/4 cup

Name that Recipe! _____ Chocolate Waffles
(HINT: breakfast recipe)

MY RECIPE

TIME	SERVES	COOK TEMP

INGREDIENTS | NOTES

DIRECTIONS

MY RECIPE

TIME	SERVES	COOK TEMP

INGREDIENTS	NOTES

DIRECTIONS

COLLECT OUR BOOKS

Book Cards

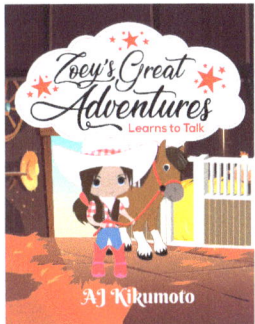
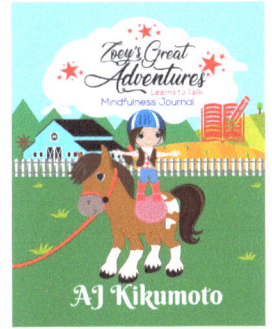

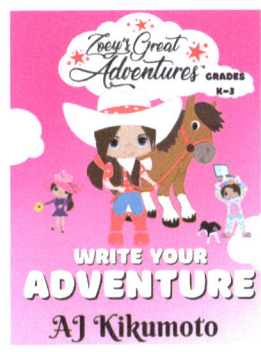
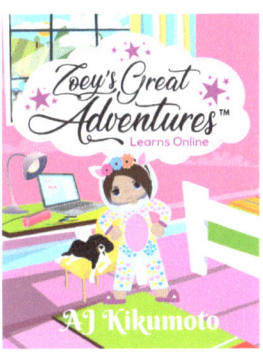

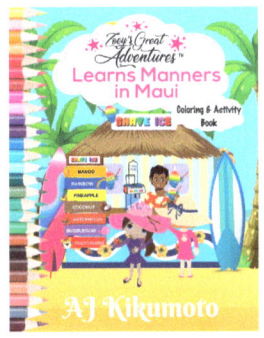

Contact for Book Readings
Hello@queenpublishingagency.com

www.QueenPublishingAgency.com

Kindly leave a favorable review and Grab a FREEbie!

1. Click on the Review Link by scanning the QR code or going to linktr.ee/AJKikumto OR
2. Log into your Amazon account.
3. Click on Your Account (3 lines)
4. Click on Your Orders: Click on the purchase of this book
5. Scroll to the bottom of the page to Customer Reviews
6. Leave a Favorable Review.
   Bonus points for sharing a Video/Photo in the Review.

RESOURCES

90 funny Christmas jokes guaranteed to sleigh kids and adults. (2022, December 9). TODAY.com. https://www.today.com/life/holidays/christmas-jokes-rcna48067

Best Basic Crêpes recipe. (2023, September 26). Delish. https://www.delish.com/cooking/recipe-ideas/recipes/a52114/easy-basic-crepe-recipe/

Fatherly. (2022, December 2). 33 Ho-ho-larious Christmas dad jokes for kids. Fatherly. https://www.fatherly.com/entertainment/funny-corny-christmas-jokes-for-kids

Nadeau, A., & Nadeau, A. (2019, December 17). 55 Christmas Themed Dad Jokes for Kids to Dial up their Holiday Spirit. The Dad. https://www.thedad.com/50-christmas-themed-dad-jokes-for-kids-to-dial-up-their-holiday-spirit/

Reindeer brownies. (2023, May 19). Taste of Home. https://www.tasteofhome.com/recipes/reindeer-brownies/

AJ Kikumoto

AJ is happily married to her adorable husband Charles and loves her job as a Mom to her beautiful six children. A master's degree in Elementary Education has served her well and inspired her to bring the STEAM aspect to this unique Holiday cookbook. As CEO of Queen Publishing Agency, she loves helping others get published and seeing their dreams come true! As a former NBA Denver Nuggets Dancer, she loves watching her kids thrive. She enjoyed writing and publishing her book "Mental Toughness for Athletes: 7 Strategies to Build Grit, Boost Emotional Resilience and Become Unstoppable." The Zoey's Great Adventures™ series has been a blast to write and publish, sharing her experiences raising six kids and the family mantra, "You Can Do Hard Things."

Aaliyah Kikumoto

Aaliyah loves her time in college at Texas Tech University and on the Pom Squad. Last year, she danced with the Dallas Cowboy Cheerleaders, and this year, she danced in the Macy's Thanksgiving Day Parade in NYC. We can't wait to find out what next year will bring! She is dabbling in some modeling gigs and having fun learning to cook and bake for her roommates. Check out the Aaliyah Kikumoto™ Dare 2 Dream Coloring book series. "Be You" and "Be Amazing" available on Amazon and other outlets. Aaliyah's favorite holiday tradition is watching movies with the family and baking and decorating sugar cookies.

Akyra Kikumoto

Akyra is loving high school and the many challenges that come along with it. She loves to bake and cook in the kitchen. Watch out! She makes a yummy cookie! She is also an avid golfer and is on the high school girl's golf team. Becoming a Black Belt at our martial arts dojo is top on her list for her next primary goal. One more belt rank and she's got it! Akyra's favorite holiday tradition is slowing down, watching Christmas movies with the family, and baking yummy cookies and candy.

 Amaya Kikumoto

Amaya is our 3rd teenager! She has a smile for days and is the sweetest little thing. Amaya is a competitive dancer; lyrical and ballet are her favorite dance styles. She is getting her toes wet in the modeling industry. NHTV is the middle school news team, and Amaya is on camera frequently in front of the whole school. Amaya's favorite Christmas traditions are putting up the Creche and decorating the tree. She loves baking cookies and delivering them to our friends and neighbors. Family movie time is a must and brings great joy.

Akayla Kikumoto

Akayla is currently our tween who is slaying it in middle school and school choir. She is a competitive dancer with a personality flowing out of her veins. She is full of sass and energy and has lots of friends. She is getting her feet wet in the modeling world and loves trying new things. Akayla's favorite Christmas traditions are making sugar cookies and decorating the gingerbread house. Relaxing with the family and watching Christmas movies is a fond memory.

CJ Kikumoto

CJ is our only boy. He is our gentle giant. He loves to play tackle football, golf, basketball, and Minecraft. He loves to try the foods we make in the kitchen and always talks about the restaurant he will run when he grows up. Be on the lookout for CJ's Burgers and Amusement Park in about 20 years. CJ's favorite traditions are eating yummy food and watching Christmas movies with his family. His favorite movie is How the Grinch Stole Christmas (cartoon version) and Elf movies. Listening to Christmas carols always makes us happy as we drive around to all our activities.

Alyvia Kikumoto

Alyvia is our baby who loves her dolls and playing with her siblings. She is also a competitive dancer, learning new acro skills like her sisters. She loves school and loves her teacher. She is also very artistic and loves coloring in our coloring & activity books. Alyvia loves her family so much. She got Alopecia when her oldest sister left for college, and she was stressed and heartbroken missing her. She is excited to decorate cookies and watch the Grinch and Polar Express movies with her family. Singing Christmas carols and decorating the Christmas tree every year brings in the spirit of Christmas, celebrating our Lord and Saviour's birth. Our Elf on the Shelf™ elf is named Abby, and Alyvia loves to see where she lands from visiting Santa every night.

Charles Kikumoto

Charles is the head of the family and brings so much joy to our lives. We call him "Disneyland Dad" as he loves his wife and children so much he is always planning trips for us. We are so blessed to have a dad who loves us so much!! He also is amazing in the kitchen and can grill the best steak you have ever had! Charles' favorite holiday tradition is being with family and watching Christmas movies.

158   S.T.E.A.M. Holiday Cookbook for Kids 4-12

S.T.E.A.M. Holiday Cookbook for Kids 4-12

www.ingramcontent.com/pod-product-compliance
Lightning Source LLC
Chambersburg PA
CBHW042053050526
44107CB00109B/1117